OUR
LEWES

OUR
LEWES

DAVID ARSCOTT

The
History
Press

First published in 2004 by
Sutton Publishing Limited

Reprinted in 2011 by
The History Press
The Mill, Brimscombe Port,
Stroud, Gloucestershire, GL5 2QG
www.thehistorypress.co.uk

British Library Cataloguing in Publication Data
A catalogue record for this book is available from
the British Library.

ISBN 978-0-7509-3664-4

Typeset in 10.5/13.5 Sabon.
Typesetting and origination by
Sutton Publishing Limited.
Printed and bound in Great Britain by
Marston Book Services Limited, Didcot

Contents

Here is a snapshot of Lewes in the words and images of local people during the summer of 2003. Those familiar with the attractive county town will enjoy teasing out the small changes that have taken place since.

Introduction

This book was born of a growing impatience. Living in one of the finest human-scale towns in the country, I have become increasingly affronted by the tendency to view it through a shimmering heritage haze – as an historical artefact rather than a thriving, dynamic community. The problem is not confined to Lewes. Authors of Sussex books (and I am a guilty party here) readily concentrate on the past, leaving our newspapers to chronicle the life of today. Even those works that feature photographs of the contemporary scene usually do so in order to contrast them, often to their detriment, with characterful views of yesteryear.

Of course, for the many of us who care about such things, the venerableness of the town's ancient buildings constitutes a real, if incalculable, part of the pleasure of living in Lewes. And by the same token, the richness of our urban experience is deepened by the knowledge of events and personalities whose dramas have been played out here: the great battle of 1264, the immolation of Protestant martyrs in the High Street, Thomas Paine debating for revolution at the White Hart. There is, however, an everyday vitality to Lewes which can be appreciated even by those only dimly aware of such things, and it is this bustling life of its shops, pubs, restaurants, schools, churches and a host of organisations of every kind that I have attempted to celebrate here: this book is a record of the here and now.

The record is presented in the words of the people themselves: apart from the briefest of notes in the captions, these are first-hand testimonies. Resurrecting two of my previous careers, as a newspaper reporter and a BBC radio producer, I have taken to the streets with notebook and microphone in hand – and a camera, too, but I make no claims in this department. If the presentation sometimes has a raw feeling to it, that is intentional: had the text been carefully crafted in a literary style, it would have appeared more polished but would have lost the refreshing immediacy of the spoken voice.

The book is organised by areas – sometimes small streets, sometimes whole estates. I have occasionally freely wandered across boundaries, and have carved up the central spine of the town (which necessarily predominates) into manageable parts. The High Street runs, properly speaking, from Cliffe Bridge to St Anne's church, but I have included the pedestrian precinct within Cliffe (as most of us do mentally in any case) and have then climbed to the prison crossroads in three stages: School Hill, as far as the war memorial; High Street from the memorial to the bottleneck; and St Anne's Hill with Western Road. I have included a smattering of uncaptioned photographs of shop signs and street furniture for readers who may like to test their powers of observation.

For each area I have found one or two guides to give an overview, and I have then trawled the streets, inspired by their comments but also giving myself licence to include anything that has taken my fancy. This is not, it should be stressed, one of those publications which demand or accept payment for inclusion: any perceived sins of omission (or inclusion) have nothing to do with financial corruption and a great deal to do with personal whim. I have attempted to present an overall sense of the experience of living in Lewes, while accepting that true comprehensiveness would be an ambition leading to madness. I have not, for instance, ventured along Mountfield Road to the football club, Priory School, tertiary college and leisure centre, although I readily acknowledge their importance. I have, on the other hand, visited three estates – Malling, Landport and the Nevill – which are all too often overlooked.

Will the book become dated? Inevitably – and as a record of Lewes during the months of July and August 2003, it will itself become a small part of the historical record. Elphicks in the Cliffe, for instance, closed during this period, and Tony Elphick is duly shown (page 13) in the doorway of his shop on the very last day of business. Other shops will disappear one by one over the years, pubs will change hands (and/or names) and the people whose voices we hear will pass on, whether literally, figuratively or both. No matter. The book has been compiled, after all, for the residents and interested visitors of today.

Few will deny that Lewes deserves eulogising. I have spoken of its human scale and perhaps should give some substance to what is admittedly a vague term. It is not a place where one becomes seriously lost: the High Street follows the crest of the downland spur and can be walked comfortably in half an hour. None of our buildings dwarfs us, even if the occasional modern monstrosity has managed to shoulder its way in. Large enough for us to steer clear of those whom we would rather avoid, the town is yet small enough for us to be confident of bumping into friends on the shortest of strolls. And should we wish to make our mark, politically or otherwise, no organisation is so vast as to swamp our individual endeavour. It is a place which encourages us to feel happy in our skins.

The final chapter is rather different from those that precede it, and I trust that I shall be forgiven a seeming self-indulgence. I have included my own home territory (St Nicholas Lane, off the war memorial), not because I regard it as superior to any other but, conversely, because of what it suggests about Lewes as a whole. Once largely a commercial area, the street is now predominantly residential. In recording that change and introducing some of today's inhabitants, this account suggests in skeletal form an alternative approach to the writing of local history – a street-by-street record of individual lives, emphasising the fascinating variety of characters who live cheek by jowl in today's Lewes. My book is dedicated to all 15,000 of them.

David Arscott, 2004

1 Cliffe

Miles Jenner

Miles is head brewer and joint managing director of Harvey's Brewery.

I was born and bred here, and in the early 1950s Cliffe really had everything you could imagine in a High Street. It was very self-sufficient, as many areas of Lewes were, with at least three greengrocers, four if you include one just round the corner in Malling street, two butchers, a fishmonger, various clothing stores, a little department store called Clements, which is on the site where Bill is now, and a betting shop. We also had the Odeon Cinema, and the street would close down at midday on Saturdays, when we children poured out after watching *Zorro* and would chase after each other waving make-believe guns.

The whole area was a sort of leftover from the Victorian age. It was always said that if you wanted anything you could go to Cliffe and get it. There were hardware

stores, Harper & Eede with their agricultural machinery, Woolworths (which is still here today) and Timothy White's. Elphicks, which closed only recently, was part of the heritage of Cliffe. In the '50s they had their seed store in Soap Factory Lane, as it was then, just round the corner in Malling Street, and as kids we would go round there to buy sacks of hay and bags of pellets for our rabbits.

Over the years fortunes changed: sometimes the top of the town would become more vibrant, and Cliffe would go into the doldrums before resurging in a slightly different form. One constant, I suppose, has been the brewery – one of five situated in Cliffe over the centuries, but the last to survive. Brewing on the banks of the Ouse we've had a certain amount of fun over the years, such as the floods in 1960 and again in 2000. Forty years on nothing much changed, except that the water was 2ft

higher and, whereas before we merrily allowed the casks to float round the brewery and then sent them out with the tide, this time we destroyed everything because public health considerations are taken much more seriously than they were.

We were brewing on the day of the 2000 flood. When we were forced to abandon the brew, we had in the fermenting room two vessels half full of strong sugars with yeast pitched in, and the last thing we did with the one remaining power supply we had was to pump the sugars from one vessel into the other to fill it up so that we could skim the yeast off. It made a beer totally unrepresentative of anything we'd brewed before, and we thought it would be great fun to bottle it and sell it in aid of the flood relief fund. Even before we announced this people were coming up to us in the street and saying 'We're all trying to decide what name to call your disaster brew, which you'll inevitably bring out, because you always do.' We'd done the same thing after the fire of 1996. It was the jeweller Simon Beer and his wife who stopped me on School Hill and said they'd all been in the pub and come up with the name Ouse Booze. I didn't think it was quite Harvey's style, but the telephone started ringing and people were saying 'When's the Ouse Booze coming out?', so I gave in. We dedicated it to our staff who had got us back into action within nine days of the flood. We had about eighty-four barrels, and we sold out within a month of Christmas. People were going out with a case under each arm, and we raised over £20,000 for the flood appeal.

Our brewery shop has gone through tremendous changes. During the 1950s we were selling spirits from the cask. They would draw them off into a bottle and you would have our own brands of spirits – Lewes Blend Whisky and things of that nature. They also sold vinegar, which came in enormous casks, and you would draw off malt vinegar into quart bottles. It was a fairly rough-and-ready shopping experience, and I don't think it was considered that we were there as serious retailers. In the early '70s we were advised by our consultants to sell the shop off because there was no way we could compete. Today it's our most successful retail outlet. We own forty-five pubs within a 50-mile radius of Lewes, but this is the top of the league. We sell over a thousand barrels of beer a year through the shop in anything from a pint to an 18-gallon container. That's been a complete turn-about during living memory.

The area is going through a very buoyant period at the moment. I try to buy whatever I can in Cliffe out of pure sentiment, and there's a good choice. Different traders come and go – and the spread of antique shops is one tremendous change within living memory – but there's more of a balance today. We now have a thriving greengrocer in our midst, for example. It's lovely to see Bill's there – apart from the fact that his tumbrils wake me up at 3 o'clock every morning as they bump over the cobble stones. He's brought a real cosmopolitan, bohemian touch to the Cliffe, and he attracts a lot of people – as does our John Harvey Tavern just behind him, which also has a continental feel to it, with people sitting outside and wandering in and out. And just over the bridge, the former Beck's garage is now the Riverside, with its food hall and a range of other shops.

Clark's Jewellers

John Clark is senior partner of W.E. Clark & Sons, which has premises on both sides of Cliffe Bridge. A former president of Lewes Chamber of Commerce, he is a member of the Lewes Flood Action group, which is lobbying for flood protection in the town.

The business started in 1819 to our knowledge, and my grandfather took over this building at 1 Cliffe High Street in 1919. We've now got the fourth generation of the Clark family involved – my son David. I purchased the shop on the other side of

the river in 1979. That sells many of the brands we market (watches, Fabergé jewellery and important gift brands such as Swarovski, Moorcroft and Bridge leather) while this shop specialises in the diamond and gem-set jewellery that we make up ourselves. We do have some traditional jewellery, but we also import nice gold modern gold jewellery from the Vicenza region of Italy, which is a gold manufacturing centre.

Diamonds are our best selling-line. We source them internationally – we've just been over to Antwerp. We also buy precious stones as near the source as we can. We meet Bangkok and Sri Lankan dealers on trips to Basle in Switzerland, and may be going out to Bangkok itself. We make up our diamond jewellery ourselves, in that we employ someone in Birmingham to do it for us, so we're able to offer good quality, style and price.

There are a lot of jewellers in Lewes, and they're all very different – second-hand specialists, designer jewellers using silver, and so on. The competition's definitely good. It's been proved in other spheres as well, that if you have a selection of similar shops in a town it is an attraction.

When we had the disastrous floods in the year 2000 Lewes District Council actively supported our regeneration. John Crawford, the chief executive, came along to meetings and asked how he could help – and he did help. Lewes was the worst affected town in Britain. Only six weeks ago Lewes Flood Action were at Defra in London, meeting the top civil servant whose job is to implement government policy on flood defences. The government has a very complicated method of apportioning money, and we suspect that this allows them to do what they want. We're very lucky in having Tom Crossett here in the town. He used to be the chief engineer at Defra in the late 1980s, and so he understands all this. He's very enthusiastically helping us try to get proper flood defences for Lewes, which is a hugely difficult thing to do. If you'll excuse the pun, we seem to be swimming against the tide all the time. After the flood the government said they'd put flood defences in, but now it's going to be an earth mound to protect Malling, and that's about it. It's simply not good enough.

I was once trying to explain how important Lewes was commercially, and a civil servant said to me that if a customer couldn't buy their watch in my shop they could just as easily go to Brighton if I didn't exist. It was perhaps said in a weak moment, but that's how the government views Lewes. It's an outrageous way of looking at things, because if Lewes does literally go down the river it would be hugely detrimental to the fairly fragile economy of East Sussex. We've got to do something about Lewes for the good of the greater area as well as just for ourselves.

Retailing in Lewes has a good future because of the town's historical past. It's an interesting place to visit, and it has a lot of smaller shops which aren't national brands. That appeals to people, because they get a little bit bored by the shopping mall concept, which means you could be anywhere between Land's End and John o' Groats. I can't see Lewes coming back from another flood like the one in 2000, but other than that I'm upbeat about the future. The town is thriving.

Tony Elphick outside Elphicks of Lewes on Saturday 26 July 2003, the day it closed after 180 years of trading. The business was founded by his great-great-grandfather.

Cliffe Bookshop

Phil and Bridget Flowers took over Cliffe Bookshop in 1991.

Lewes is a very bookish kind of town. We do especially well with literary novels, biography, poetry and local books. There's a lot of competition from Brighton shops and the Internet, but thankfully we've built up a supportive and loyal customer base over the years, including authors and illustrators, actors and MPs – even a former prime minister. We've also held a good many book events, signings and launches.

After the floods of 2000 we were evacuated for several days, and when we got back we found that most of the stock was covered in flood water and the rest was ruined by damp – everything was written off. The building had to be gutted from floor to ceiling, and we were out of business for fifty weeks. Our home is above and behind the shop, so we had to move out, too.

For a time it looked as if we would never reopen, but we realised that we were in a position to split the shop, letting off the other half, and that made the business more sustainable. We'd already been hit very hard by the ending of the net book agreement. Before that it didn't matter if you were little old Cliffe Bookshop or W.H. Smith, you sold books at the price on the cover, but the change made things tougher for us: it's not a level playing field, because the big chains are given discounts not available to small shops like us.

Having said that, we do have some advantages. We have a wide range of stock, and we're able to offer a speedy ordering service. On top of that, it's a pleasure to be surrounded by books all day – and be at work!

Fur, Feathers 'n' Fins

Sue Field has been running the corner pet shop with her husband Paul for the past thirteen years.

He looks after the dry goods and the business side, while my side of it is the animals. We've got quite a range, from rats, hamsters and gerbils to spiders and scorpions. We have snakes, but just the occasional hognose, because they're the only ones that won't attack me. I had a dreadful fight with a 10ft python which someone delivered in a 6ft converted sideboard.

We've had chinchilla and chipmunk fashions, but at the moment everyone seems to be going for rats. They're lovely creatures. Apart from cats and dogs they're the only pets that will really show you affection – although they'll also turn their back on you if they're not pleased with you. They're domesticated, and so don't have the natural fight and flight instincts, and they tend not to bite.

I'm very careful who I sell to. I ask where people live and why they've chosen a particular kind of pet. Terrapins used to be popular, but customers needed to be told that although they start less than an inch across, they end up the size of dinner plates. I'll refuse to sell to people I don't think are suitable, and they can get pretty angry about that. I'll find myself reported to the RSPCA for some imaginary offence. In fact I've got very good relationships with local vets. Animals always come first with me.

No, I don't want to be photographed, thank you. Take a picture of my Chinese Crested, Fraggle.

Bill's Produce Store

Bill Collison set up a greengrocer's business with his father in Cliffe some twenty years ago, and his wife Rebecca later helped him build it up into a delicatessen and café – but without the floods of 2000, Bill says, the final transformation into a modern Lewes phenomenon might never have taken place at all.

We had this vision. We had an ideas file we'd been building up – what we'd be proud of doing so that we could go home at night and say 'that was great'. And that's what we did. The flood allowed us to rethink everything. I always knew that if you made something really nice, as long as it wasn't overpriced, then people would use you. We thought the money would follow, to make the thing feasible, and that took about a year. Now it's fabulous.

I sourced out from friends in the fresh produce trade, and we got some good supplies from Thailand and other Asian countries, and one thing leads to another.

As soon as you get a new supplier you find that other companies from the same country are on the phone to you – you're inundated with samples. You have to get that foot in the door first, and then it leads to other countries and suddenly they all want to send to you, and that's really nice. We get stuff from all round the world, direct from growers and manufacturers, from small businesses in Thailand and India that make jams, jellies and chutneys.

But it's really a success because both my wife and I are in love with what we do. As soon as the romance goes we'll pack it up.

We have a vast amount of wild mushrooms. I've got ten different kinds of cucumber in the shop today and twenty different types of tomato. It astounds me how many people buy these things. They try them, and they realise how fascinating they are and what different flavours they have, and they come back and buy them again. The people of Lewes are adventurous in their cooking. I wouldn't have believed it, but elderly people – those you wouldn't dream would be interested – they'll try the food and come back. The food programmes on TV have made a lot of difference.

Fresh produce has a limited life, of course, but this is where the café comes in. It's an amazing business, because it goes round in a circle. The chef won't use anything unless it's really good and ripe. As soon as it gets ripe he takes it from the shop and cooks it in the kitchen. Something that's worth £1 there is worth £2 when you cook it – so something you might otherwise have to throw away makes you even more money.

The people of Lewes have been fabulous towards me. The support I got after the flood – just giving me that chance – because you can open a new business and it will fail if it isn't absolutely right. I felt that whatever I did they'd give me that chance, because they knew that I was a Lewes dad, they knew that we were feeling miserable because we'd lost our home and everything in the flood, and they really got behind us. They've been the same ever since – brilliant, really brilliant.

A view along Cliffe High Street from the bridge with Bill's at no. 56.

Above: Pub signs for the Gardener's Arms and the John Harvey Tavern.

St Thomas's church in the Cliffe.

The Riverside

Cade Craft

Henry Cade and his wife Cynthia set up Cadecraft twenty years ago. He's researched the history of the Riverside building.

This is one of the oldest wooden commercial buildings still in use anywhere in the country. It was formerly a garage, and Ford Ts were winched up here to the top floor where we have our shop. During the war gas masks were made here. You used to be able to hire rowing boats outside, and there's a key in the town hall which anyone can ask for if they want to open the gate and launch a boat on the Ouse. Not many people know that!

The Riverside's been a great success. We've been in business for twenty years and moved here from the top of town six years ago. It was definitely the right decision. Our biggest lines are haberdashery and fabrics, but we've sold a lot of wool since the wool shop in the High Street closed. We're also one of the few places left where you can bring in your sewing machine for repair.

Say Cheese

David and Eleanor Robins were among the first occupants of the Riverside Centre, having previously owned a cheese shop in Herstmonceux. Eleanor says they're very happy with Lewes.

They're our kind of people, by which I mean interested, 'foody' and loyal to anything British and particularly anything produced locally. When we started out that was our point of difference. Although we sell cheese from all over the world we wanted to promote what was made locally. We're very lucky in Sussex in having a couple of the most skilled cheesemakers anywhere today – the Blunts in Golden Cross and the Harveys at Duddleswell. They win prizes on a regular basis, including international prizes. There aren't many cheesemakers in Hampshire, there's one notable small firm in Surrey and a sprinkling in Kent – but Sussex is lousy with them!

We can't be stopped from talking about food, because it's our passion. It's wonderful here in the Riverside, with a butcher next to us, a fishmonger opposite and a brewery across the road – what more could we want? This is the place to come for proper food, raw food, stuff that hasn't been processed and whose origins we know. I know the goats, the sheep, the cows. I can talk to you about them until they come home.

Eleanor Robins (left) with her assistant Joy Hazell and a few of their many cheeses.

Colin Staplehurst, butcher

Colin Staplehurst managed Pryor's butcher's shop in the High Street for twenty years before moving down to the Riverside Centre to run his own business.

I was doing quite well until the floods, and it's taken me two years to build it back up again. With 600 houses flooded, most of my customers had gone elsewhere. I do get people coming from a distance, but that was a real blow.

The Riverside Centre is a lovely place to be in – a very friendly atmosphere. The High Street has some very good shops, but it doesn't work if you're the only food shop there. You need a range.

Our free-range pork is very popular. People come a long way for that. But I specialise in sausages, and I'm known for creating some unusual ones. We had pork with baked beans and two cheeses the other day. They were fantastic. For the golden jubilee I used food dye to make red, white and blue sausages.

The Atkins diet has been good for butchers recently. We're selling a lot of rump steak, because they can eat as much of that as they like. In the last eight weeks I sold forty rumps.

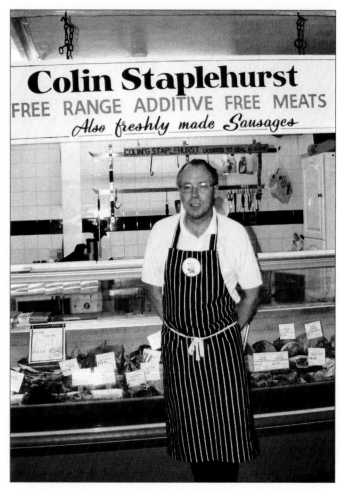

Terry's Fish Bar

Lee Webster was born and bred in Newhaven, and that's where he gets most of the fish he sells from his shop in the Riverside Centre.

We buy as much local fish as we can, and about three-quarters of it comes from Newhaven – cod, plaice, sole and so on. I go down to the fish market early in the morning, at about four, and pick out exactly what we want. The catches are very poor these days and they're getting worse. If you go back ten years, the boats would

land about thirty-five boxes of fish a day, but now it's probably twenty a day at most. It is getting quite bad down there. Cod is dropping away especially badly, but everything's short. The fish is getting more expensive, but it's still good value and you can find some bargains – dabs and fresh sardines are still very cheap.

The people of Lewes are knowledgeable, and they'll try new things. They'll often ask how to cook something, and we try to give them a recipe. We're selling more and more exotic fish such as swordfish and tuna these days. We get those sent down from Billingsgate, and we bring in Scottish haddock and salmon, too.

I eat fish three or four days a week, and my own particular favourite is skate. I absolutely love it.

A farmers' market is held on the first Saturday of every month in the pedestrian precinct.

FITZROY HOUSE

FORMER MEMORIAL LIBRARY
TO HON. HENRY FITZROY M.P.
FOR LEWES 1837-1860. BUILT
1862 BY HIS WIDOW
(ARCHITECT SIR
GEORGE GILBERT
SCOTT,) IT STANDS
ON PART OF THE
SITE OF THE
GREY FRIARS
(DISSOLVED 1538)   19 83

NEXT

THIS STORE IS NOW CLOSED

YOUR NEAREST NEXT
STORES ARE AT
BRIGHTON
AND
EASTBOURNE.

WE APOLOGISE FOR ANY
INCONVENIENCE CAUSED

2 Landport

George Oakley & Harry Sunderland

George and Harry, now in their late seventies, are both former chairmen of the Landport Residents Association. George, a fence erector, came to the estate in the 1950s. Harry, a mechanical engineer, arrived in the 1970s.

G: When I applied to the council for a bigger house and they found me one at Landport I wasn't too happy about coming here, because Landport did have a dodgy name in those days – nobody wanted to come here. But having been here all this time and having, as you might say, got among the people, I can say that they're among the best in Lewes. It's the friendliest estate of the lot. I worked for the council for many years, and to me, as a workman going to people's houses all over the area, it always seemed the best estate to work on. There was less animosity.

H: My wife and I lived in a village near Horsham for a time before we came here. When you get to a village you're a foreigner and people don't want to know. My

Landport lies on the Greenwich Meridian line. This column was erected in Meridian Road in October 1938, to commemorate the development of the estate.

missus would go in the village shop and everyone would stop talking. It was totally different when we came to Landport. People were friendly from the start.

G: We've got a very good corner shop here. They'll get in anything they think people might want. It's the nearest thing you'll get to the old-fashioned village shop that used to keep everything from a bag of nails to a packet of peanuts. It has a post office, too, and even people from the middle of town use it. There's a good bus service from the centre, every twenty minutes. You pick it up outside Safeway, and it stops right outside the shop.

The estate is almost twice as big as when I first came because of all the building. They've done a lot for the old people here.

H: Yes, they've made a good job of the old people's places. There are some bungalows along Newton Road, with a lovely communal room. I've always argued that we need good affordable housing, but I did try to keep eighty-eight garages that I thought we needed. The Guinness Trust eventually built nine houses on the site, but I thought there were other places they could have put them and I fought tooth and nail to keep those garages. Now, of course, we could do with them.

G: We've still got a small community room on the estate. We had two shops originally, but one of them never really took off. They tried to start a fish and chip takeaway in the building, and then there was an idea of turning it into a launderette, but the drainage system wasn't good enough, so what they've done is create what they call a resource centre. There's a room that will take about forty people and a council office, although that's not manned all the time. The person who runs it is what they call a tenant participation officer, who's a sort of mentor for resident associations throughout the town. We can't hold proper parties at the centre, because there's an embargo on it after half past nine at night, but we do sometimes have meetings there.

George (left) and Harry in George's garden.

H: Something else I fought for was a football pitch next to the school. When the old Pells junior school closed down in Talbot Terrace – that's over the bridge in the Pells area – they moved it in with the infant school here, and what used to be their playing field had extra buildings put on it. There was plenty of topsoil thrown up when the building work was going on, and I thought it could be used to level out a piece of ground next to it so the kids would have a decent pitch to play on. I rang the architect, who was quite happy about it, but he needed a note from the council to say it was okay, and the buggers wouldn't do it. I found a chap who would do it for under £2,000, but I couldn't get the go-ahead.

G: There's too much apathy about, despite the fact that it's a friendly place, but some things do get done. Take the Tally Ho – the pub's in the best state it's been for years. The landlord Dick is a bloke who knows what his business is about. He's just refurbished it, with a new bit on the back – the old off-licence has been taken into the building to make a function room. The pub is well used by the estate, and that's just what we've needed.

H: We used to have a farm here, and my son worked there for a time. Now it's been turned into a care home. We do still have quite a number of allotments, though, and they seem to be pretty well used.

Landport Allotments

Anne Bostwick has been on the committee of the allotments association.

I've had my half-plot for seven years. It costs me £14 a year, which is very, very cheap. I don't live at Landport – I'm from the Wallands Estate. In fact I don't think many people here do live on the Landport. There's quite a mixture.

We used to have a problem with kids getting in and causing a bit of damage, but it's not so bad now that we have padlocks on the gates. Couch grass is my main problem at the moment, because I've been ill and haven't been able to do as much as I'd like. When you're down here you're pleased to meet somebody, because it's hard work and you're quite relieved to stop and chat. Allotments seem to be popular at the moment. People are taking early retirement and some of them have more time on their hands.

Bill Dumbrell has had his 10-rod plot at Landport for about twenty years.

I've lived in Lewes since I was a boy, and I was always keen on gardening. My father and my uncle were gardeners, so I've followed in their footsteps, and now my two sons are following me. One's a jobbing gardener, who shares the allotment with me, and the other is the kitchen gardener at the Newick Park Hotel.

It's a very nice community on the allotments. Everybody is very friendly. I've got spuds, onions, raspberries, fennel, courgettes . . . . We have an allotment association which meets periodically and asks the council to do things for us – which sometimes they do! A few of the plots aren't being used, but most are well tended. It's very popular down here.

Landport Stores

Sunny Patel joined his brother Naresh and sister-in-law Nalini at Landport in 1985, four years after they opened the business, and is now a familiar face in the store.

We started with just a general store, with newspapers and groceries plus a post office, and then we got an off-licence. We try our best to get anything people want. We've a customer who comes from the Hailsham area, for instance. She comes just to buy a special type of sauce that we do. It's a sour chutney sauce she can't get anywhere else. She's an English lady, not an Asian, and she says she can't get it any more where she lives.

We had a robbery at gunpoint two years back in October when Mrs Patel was on the till. I was out the back getting some fireworks. The person came in with a gun and took the cash. We called the cops and they were very quick. We identified the person, but the police never managed to catch him. I can't understand why that was, but he's left the estate now, and we never see him.

I'm down here from 5 o'clock in the morning, because that's when we expect the main delivery, and the papers come at 5.30. The shop door is open. While I'm doing the work I might as well serve people, and the customers will help me offloading papers or anything if I get busy. We close at 7 o'clock, and then we'll sometimes go to the cash-and-carry. We're very happy here in this small community.

Naresh and Nalini Patel with sub-postmistress Linda Ongley and their daughters Mira (centre) and Payal (right). Mira was one month old when the family – driven out of Uganda during the dictatorship of Idi Amin – came to Lewes. Sunny asked not to appear in the picture.

Pells Church of England Primary School

Valerie Cobb has been headteacher for five years.

We're a voluntary controlled church school, so we do a lot with the church and the local community. At least 90 per cent of the Landport children come to our school. Many of their parents and grandparents came here before them, so there's a lot of history embedded within the school – something I didn't realise when I came here.

The people within the local area are extremely supportive. We've a very active family club, which has won national and international awards for the projects they've completed. A lot of parents take part in events, and so do other local people – those in the flats close to the school, for instance. They've been active in building our wildlife area, which featured on the BBC recently. Several companies have sponsored the project, and the children, staff, parents and local residents maintain it.

Before I came here in January 1998 there had been a succession of acting headteachers. At that time the junior school was in a cold Victorian building in the Pells, while the infants had a bright purpose-built school on this site. The school needed strong leadership and a vision for the future, and putting all the school on one site helped immensely. The new building was finished in September 2000.

A lot of the children come from large families, so it's important for the parents to be able to see what happens as their children go through the school from the ages of four to eleven. We give them lots of opportunities to get involved in the life of the school, and a hard-working Friends of Pells fundraises for us.

Our next development will be the introduction of a breakfast club and after-school child care in the youth centre along the road each weekday. The doors will open at 8 o'clock – some of the children come to school without having had breakfast – and will close at 6 o'clock in the evening. These innovations will be very helpful for working parents.

There's a good family atmosphere in the school, and our SATs results are fantastic in showing the children's achievements in terms of value-added progress. We've won national awards, such as the Artsmark gold award, which is for drama, music, dance and art, and we've also been awarded the Basic Skills Quality Mark for Numeracy and Literacy. The 2002 Ofsted report said that 'Pells is a good school with very good and excellent features,' and it added that 'there is an excellent shared commitment to improve and succeed.'

Yes, it's a very happy ship.

Jamie Knight and Rasiqah Zulkifli with the Archdeacon of Lewes, the Venerable Nicholas Reed, at the opening of the combined infant and junior school.

Mary may have had a little lamb, but the Pells School children had bullocks as companions for a time when the floods of 2000 swept away their fencing.

3 Friars Walk & Lansdown Place

Jo Bentley

Managing editor of the Book Guild in Lewes, Jo Bentley lives at 1 Friars Walk with her husband Mark (a sub-editor with the Mid-Sussex Times*) and their two children.*

This is a main route between the town centre and the railway station, so it's used by a lot of people, although not all of them get a chance to stop and look around. It's a mainly residential area, but the street is quietly commercial, too, with a hobby shop, interiors and antiques shops, takeaways and the cosiest sweet shop I know. Florence's is tiny, but has a great stock of sweets, including jars of old-fashioned things like cough candies and bonbons. It's like a honey pot at the end of the school day.

Also at the top of Lansdown Place is Academy Music, which always has beautiful violins in the window – both classy, traditional ones and funkily modern ones. There's a lot of music in this street and you'll often hear a trumpeter practising, people singing and pianos and guitars playing. About halfway up the road is the All Saints Centre, which is a really vital youth and arts venue in the town – well used and in a great position. It's home to the Musicians of All Saints and to Lewes Film Club, among others, and it regularly hosts concerts, exhibitions and films. The hall's used by lots of local groups, and for children's workshops and after-school activities.

This is also quite an arty street. There's the Hesketh Pottery, where they have bold displays of work by local craftspeople, and on certain days you can walk past and see a lesson in progress. For Artwave, the celebration of local artists held every year at the end of the summer, the All Saints churchyard gets filled with marvellous colourful creations, like the dazzling totem pole that attracted lots of attention from passers-by one year.

As you walk up the street you can make out the origins of many of the homes. In between short stretches of Victorian terraces there are several houses that started out as shops and which still have large display windows in their front rooms. When we first moved here nearly twelve years ago, a neighbour told us that the attics of one stretch of terraced houses were all linked, and that you could walk from house to house under the roofs! Our flat is in what was originally the Railway Inn, built in the 1840s when the station was just behind Friars Walk. The board where the pub's name would have been painted, and the iron bars for a hanging sign are still fixed to the front wall.

This is a great spot for combining the benefits of town and country. While Safeway is only a thirty-second sprint away (if I realise halfway through cooking that I've forgotten a vital ingredient), we're also just a stone's throw from the nature reserve at the Railway Land. It's a lovely area for walking, taking the children to look at frogs and birds, or to pick blackberries.

Another fabulous treat about living here is that we get a brilliant view of the processions that come past on bonfire night. For most of the evening there are streams of people walking down the middle

of the road (on a rare and lovely traffic-free night) from the station towards the town centre. Then the tide changes direction when the societies go off to their fire sites. Cliffe is always spectacular, and I make sure I'm at the front window to feel the heat from the torches every year. They come back past the house at about midnight, still playing 'Sussex by the Sea'.

Friends Meeting House

Maurice Burge has been a member of the Lewes Quakers' meeting since 1989.

I'd been interested in the Quaker movement for many years because of the peace aspect, and I thought about coming along as soon as I moved to Lewes from Hurstpierpoint, but it took me a year to pluck up the courage to cross the threshold. That was ridiculous! This is a place where you're accepted for yourself. It's completely non-judgmental. There aren't any expectations, and you feel at home very quickly.

Nobody runs it. There's a clerk who looks after the business side, and once a month we have a business meeting. Some of the Quaker business method has been taken over outside the movement. For instance, the clerk has to get 'the sense of the meeting', because we can't move forward until everyone is in agreement. Quakers don't vote, you see, because they think that always leaves a disgruntled minority. It makes business slow, but it's secure because everybody has agreed to what's

going to happen. If you can't get an agreement you'll leave it and perhaps bring it back another time when people have had time to think about it. The Quaker idea is not that you get a consensus but that there might be a divine leading, that something might occur to you as a group that nobody has thought of individually.

As for our religious practices, it's easier to say what we don't have – no symbols of any kind, no clergyman, no music and so on. Some Quakers wouldn't call themselves Christians, but we're all very aware of our Christian roots. Some would think of themselves as a fringe of Christianity. I suppose we're a slightly mystic wing of Christianity. We're nearer to the fringes of other religions than we are to the fundamentalists of our own. I went to a Quaker weekend on Sufiism, when three Sufis told us about their ideas, and because Quaker religion is silent they had no problem about joining us!

The interior of the meeting house has changed little since the late eighteenth century.

A lot of people in the nonconformist world wouldn't consider us as Christians because we're not interested in the theology of the Trinity and so on. We regard such things as 'notions'. There's a Quaker saying, 'Christ said this and the apostles said that: what do you say?' The fundamental thing is your own experience and how you put it into practice.

Quakers were persecuted by nonconformists as well as by the established Church in the past. One member of our meeting makes it her witness at bonfire time to attend both mass at the Catholic church and the Protestant service at the Jireh chapel. She knows there's antipathy there, so she goes to both sides, as it were, and she announces why she's come.

Two modern sculptures in All Saints churchyard.

The redundant All Saints church has for several years been a home to the arts in Lewes.

The water fountain in Friars Walk.

The view along Lansdown towards Station Street.

Shops at the west end of Lansdown: Wyborns, Florence's sweet shop and Academy Music.

Academy Music

Robert Haydon-Clark is a professional violinist – for twenty years a first violinist with the London Symphony Orchestra – director of the Consort of London and a violin teacher. He took over his shop some five years ago.

Lewes has a strong musical tradition. My customers come from the east as far as Rye and the west as far as Winchester, and because Academy Music specialise in string instruments, especially the violin, people come to us for our professional guidance. We also restore and value instruments as well as sell them.

It's a most productive town for children learning musical instruments, especially the violin. This year alone in the state schools there are about a hundred children starting the violin. Obviously some will give up, and others may go on to other instruments. The county have done a fantastic job. They also run Saturday morning music school at Priory, and there are youth orchestras both here and in Brighton.

Lewes has attracted many professional musicians who prefer to live here rather than in London. It's easy to commute, we're near Gatwick Airport and many of them work at Glyndebourne. There are a lot of amateur musicians, too.

Then there are the makers. I think there are five guitar makers here, which is rather unusual for an English town, to say the least. There's also a Russian violin maker living here, and in Cliffe there are people producing harpsichords.

Although we specialise in strings, we try to cater for the educational side of music, whatever the instrument. We have music for piano, violin, woodwind and brass, as well as all the accessories.

People sometimes imagine that music is a middle-class pursuit, but in this county it's very much across the board – children from all backgrounds are learning. The county music service has instruments available for families of limited means, while we usually have a range of cheaper instruments and also operate a buy-back scheme.

My aim as director of Academy Music – both as a dealer and a teacher – is to help produce as many violinists as possible in East Sussex.

Hanging signs in Lansdown: Academy Music (top) and Wyborns.

4 Station Street

Cynthia Parrott

Cynthia has run the Garden Room Café-Gallery in Station Street for the past thirteen years after twenty-three years' teaching at Henfield primary school. A feature of her café is the artwork on the walls.

I wanted it to be more of an art gallery than it's become, but now that we have Artwave in the town and people selling their work from their homes there's not such a demand. I display paintings by artists whose work I like and, yes, it's for sale. I'm not an artist myself, but I like creative people and creative work.

We do well enough, but not as well as we used to do, because we haven't got the passing trade any more. Why would you come to Station Street unless you're in a car going out of town? The noise and pollution is really quite nasty. Round the corner in the high street there used to be several food shops, including a fishmonger, a butcher's and a greengrocer's, but the top end has died down. It's because of Tesco, I think. If you come from out of Lewes and park at Tesco, by the time you've shopped there and perhaps done the riverside walk down to the Cliffe, well 'thank you very much', you've done all you're going to do in Lewes and so you go straight home again.

My shop was a wool shop before I took it over, but I've a photograph which shows that it was a café just after the First World War. There have been all sorts of changes since I opened here. On one side of me was the La Cucina restaurant, which Pepe made very successful. It became Stoyan a couple of years ago, and now it's being sold again. Next door on the other side was a sports shop. I bought it with my son, and he ran it as a sandwich shop, but he's moved into Brighton: now it's a place which supplies weddings and parties and which will cook food for you if you don't want to prepare it yourself.

The Lansdown on the corner below me used to be a good working-class pub, but I think the new owner has tried to upgrade it a bit, and it's now called the White

Star. There was a garage up the road not very long before I came here, and I've a café sign which originally had 'Ford' written on it: I salvaged it from a rubbish heap. Now it's old people's flats. It seems an odd place for them, on a hill – I certainly won't choose to go there when I'm seriously old. Further up there's the old chapel, which is now an antiques centre with lots of little stalls. There's a charity shop in what used to be Kangaroo, selling quality wools, until they moved to the High Street and then closed. (It's been replaced there by one of those shops with windows which don't reveal quite what they're selling, although I'm told that it's terribly nice.) The second-hand book shop on the corner with the High Street is new, too.

Opposite me we've the Brudditz chocolate shop started by Vic, who's well known for running the café on the railway station: he won the accolade of being the best station cafe in the region. Further up, the Jevoncraft shop is another one that's appeared since I came here.

But it's a bit of a dead street really, and it's time I started a new project. Any ideas?

A mixed bag at the bottom of Station Street west side: the Jehovah's Witnesses' Kingdom Hall, the Equilibrium fitness club, a video shop, the Brudditz chocolate shop and a hairdresser's.

The Antiques Centre on Station Street.

Lewes station.

White Star Inn

Marcus Warland turned the former Lansdown Arms into the White Star Inn early in 2001 after looking for premises that would allow him to display his collection of cruise ship memorabilia.

We spent quite a bit of money doing the place up. It had been shut down, and the police were worried about what it might become, because it hadn't been, shall we say, quite what Lewes needed. Some things had happened here that shouldn't have done, and I gave them assurance that this was going to change – by making

it a predominantly real ale pub, with no sport and only low background music. It's a meeting house to sit down and chat.

We own forty years of the lease. It was the very last Whitbread pub partnership in the whole country. Enterprise Inns have bought the firm which took over Whitbread, but I won't let them change the Whitbread signs out the front and put their own up. We've a partial tie, that's all.

I made it clear that I wouldn't take the place over with the old name because of the reputation it had. I had all the stuff to go in it – a fair few pictures and some original White Star material, which had come my way through my grandfather, who worked for Cunard. A lot of it had been handed down to me. Changing the name signalled a fresh start.

It was hard at first. People came in thinking it would be just as before, and I made it clear that they wouldn't be welcome if they were behaving in the old way. A lot of the locals didn't like it, but a fair percentage have come back and recognised the pub for what it is, together with others who wouldn't have set foot in the place before.

We get passing trade from the trains. In summer time there are a lot of people from Glyndebourne, including the singers and the staff that work there. They'll take us in on the way to the station and then again on the way back. We're in the Camra guides, and I'm a member of the Guild of Master Cellarmen, and that proves we've a bit of quality with our real ales. It's gone very well. We've astounded the brewers, who were doubtful that we'd pull it off.

We're here to stay. My wife and I have three children, and our five-year-old is well settled at Western Road school. It's a beautiful town and a good one for the children.

THE COMPANY RESPECTFULLY APPEALS TO THE FREQUENTERS OF THIS ROOM TO OBSERVE MODERATION AND GOOD FELLOWSHIP, AND TO DISCOUNTENANCE HIGH PLAY, OBJECTIONABLE LANGUAGE, AND EVERY OTHER ABUSE OF THE PURPOSE FOR WHICH THE ROOM IS PROVIDED.
WHITE STAR LINE   MARCH 1910

Jevoncraft

*Philip and Corrinne Jevon opened their art and craft shop in Station Street
seven years ago. The original idea as for Corrinne to run the business by herself,
but Philip explains that it simply grew too big.*

We cater for more than seventy crafts, from rubber stamping, glass painting,
jewellery-making, rubber-moulding, to casting, teabag-folding – which is a bit like

origami. We've hundreds of types of beads,
although not as many as we'd like. We've
tried just about everything ourselves. If people
ask you questions it's very difficult to answer
them properly if you haven't actually done it
yourself.

We're fairly central for a large catchment
area. We regularly get people in from as far
Hastings and Tunbridge Wells. A woman
jumped on the train from Oxford especially
to visit us, because there are very few shops
like this, stocking pretty well everything.
There's nothing like it in London. We also
get people coming from South Africa: they
stock up with things
and take them back.
Even things they
can get out there
are very expensive.

Card-making is
incredibly popular at the moment. No matter how many
card shops there are, people not only don't want to pay
the money, but they get the satisfaction of creating real
works of art. There are some very clever people out
there.

MORE THAN
70
CREATIVE
REASONS
TO VISIT
The BEST
ART
&
CRAFT
SHOP in
SUSSEX
JEVONCRAFT 2
29 STATION STREET
LEWES, EAST SUSSEX. BN7 2DB
phone/fax: 01273 487678
email jevoncraft@aol.com

5 Fisher Street

Marvin Cox

Born in Lewes in 1947, Marvin started working at his current premises in 1964 and bought it with his business partner, Andy Donovan, twenty-seven years ago. Marvin's wife runs Florence, the sweet shop in Lansdown Place.

I've seen a lot of changes in Lewes, with the advent of various supermarkets and the loss of many small businesses, not to speak of the increased traffic. And the place isn't as safe as it was twenty years ago. A lot of people have moved in from outside.

When I first worked in Fisher Street, if you started from McCartney and Stewarts on the corner, which is now Ask, you came to Stanleys the opticians and Seymours the electricians, which is still there today. After the council offices and the Star Brewery (which had become a store for Beard's Brewery and is now the Star Gallery) there was the fish and chip shop at no. 7; Briggs the television people; Payne's, a little sweet shop; Griffiths, the cobbler; and Guernsey Dairy, right opposite us. Then on our side of the road, from the police station corner, you had Cullens the grocers; Tappin, the electrical engineer; Bert Coombes' old-fashioned sweet shop; the blacksmith's, where Ben Stevens worked; and Brinkhurst's fruit and veg where Swanborough Nurseries is today. I remember when Mrs Brinkhurst was here and she'd cook all the beetroots up round the back. Next door to us on the other side, where the Dil Raj is now, was Beard's office and main off licence before you came to the Lamb Inn and the town hall.

We used to be the main barber's shop in Lewes. Andy and I are in here at 7.30 every morning, and 6 o'clock on Saturdays, and there are often customers waiting at the door. With the greengrocer's and the fish and chip shop we're among the three surviving originals. Small shops have managed to keep going at this end of the street. There are two other hairdressers apart from us. Donald on the corner has been there for years, while Simon over the road came here from West Street. They cater mainly for ladies. We all get on very well. In fact there's still a community spirit in the street. When I go home I'll call in for a take-away or for fish and chips, and I know most of the people here. We'll go to the Lamb, and sit out in the garden during the summer, and there's also the Lewes Arms close by in Castle Ditch Lane – that's a great pub.

C.H. Seymour

Arthur Snell started an electrical retailer's business with Colin Seymour in Seaford, and came to Fisher Street in 1961 to open C.H. Seymour. He still works on a part-time basis and plans to retire in 2004.

This building was originally a pub called the Postboy's Arms. My father-in-law used to court a young lady in here! That wall there is one of the originals. Later it became Cecil Rugg's garage and cycle shop – he was here before moving down to Station Street.

The white goods business hasn't changed much over the years. We've always sold refrigerators and cookers. We never got involved with television, because that's another entity altogether. But in the early days the contracting really mushroomed, and this branch was one of the biggest. We used to do the police, the county council and Lewes District Council. We still have a big contracting staff.

We used to repair an awful lot of things, because they were built to last, but nowadays people don't want to bother. They just throw it away. Some of the jobs

we get in here are quite interesting – they save them up for when I come in. I get a great kick out of that. More things are worth repairing than people think, although labour costs sometimes prevent it. But it's always worth asking.

Our business is run on the idea of giving personal service. You saw that lady come in just now with a problem, and I told her that if she really couldn't sort it out I'd go over to Newick to help her. If I was going out that way I'd be very pleased to do it. That goes a long way. People remember things like that, and they come back. The personal touch is still the important thing in a town like Lewes.

Michael and Pat Cooper, Star Gallery

Pat Cooper and her artist husband Michael were among the founders of the Star Gallery, which runs along Fisher Street with its entrance in Castle Ditch Lane. During the 1980s the former bottling store of Beard's Brewery was due to be turned into apartments, but a group of campaigners won the battle to turn it into artists' workshops.

There was a clamour for space right from the start. As each studio was finished we let it, even if they had to walk across gangplanks to get to their front door. Some of those people are still here fifteen years later. We've got artists, bookbinders, potters, jewellers, a shoe designer and maker, a lute and guitar maker, graphic designers and architects. It's been a great success and we always have a long waiting list.

It was what Lewes needed. Yes, Lewes is an artistic place, but we've encouraged that, and we've brought artists into the area from outside – one came down from London to live in Lewes precisely because of this place. Not only that, but we helped to start Artwave, with Carol Buchan.

The public can come in here and wander round. If a door's open they're welcome to go into the studios – if it's shut, then obviously the people need some peace and quiet. As well as the studios we have a large open area on the ground floor. In the early days it was used for storage, but the aim was always to turn it into a gallery. We had our first exhibition there in 1989, showing whatever the tenants were making at the time. As time went on we spread out to invite other local artists to show their work if we liked it, and now we have contacts with London galleries and show artists from throughout the country. We have a national reputation.

Since we refurbished the gallery about three years ago we've had exhibitions of major artists such as Picasso, Matisse, Henry Moore, Sir Hugh Casson, Andy Warhol, Alan Jones and Lucien Freud.

Michael and Pat Cooper outside the Star Gallery.

Mohamed Hamid, Star Gallery

The potter Mohamed Hamid was one of the first artists to take space at the Star Gallery. He came from Africa, trained in Surrey and worked at Drusilla's, near Alfriston, for three years before opening his workshop in Lewes.

My pottery is very traditional, classic. It's based on Italian, Spanish and Islamic ceramics, so it's brightly coloured painting on white background. I do a lot of lettering as well. It's all hand-thrown.

Lewes is an amazing centre. I would say a lot of it stems from Brighton. Many artists are attracted there, and Brighton has a fantastic college which does a really good craft and design course – several people in this building are graduates from Brighton. One of the wonderful things about the building is that is has public access. On the way through to the gallery people come into my workshop. I also advertise it as a showroom space.

The economics of commissioning individual pieces? Well, I make mugs and I can't compete with factory products. They start at 50p and I sell them for between £9 and £14. But on the larger pieces, such as bowls, potters can quite comfortably compete. I have no middle men, no distributors, no agents for selling my work. In addition I do specialised lettering work – I've done it for Glyndebourne, for the district council and for individuals, too. I hand-letter my work for specialist events such as birthdays and weddings.

Mohamed at work at the Star Gallery.

Rachel Ward-Sale, Star Gallery

Rachel Ward-Sale has been bookbinding at the Star Galley since 1992 with her colleague Gill.

We do a lot of work for universities, binding the Ph.D. students' theses, as well as repairs, rebinds, albums, box-making and general bookbinding. The bookshops recommend us to people who want their old copies bound, so we get quite a bit of trade passed on from them. The cost of cloth binding is quite reasonable, but leather's expensive.

One of the most satisfying jobs is repairing family Bibles. They look really nice when they're finished, and we always seem to have one or two on the go. Usually the boards have fallen off, so we re-attach the boards to the book and put a new piece of leather over the spine. We then either put the old spine back on or, if it's missing, tool it up as close to the original as we can.

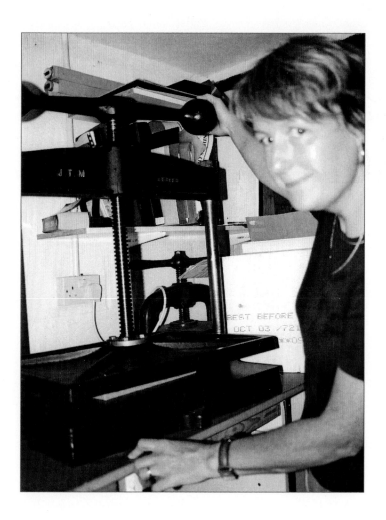

Two popular Lewes pubs in close proximity: the Lamb in Fisher Street and the Lewes Arms in Castle Ditch Lane.

Ben Autie, blacksmith

Ben Autie trained in art but worked at the forge in Offham until, twenty years ago, his present premises came on to the market.

I do all sorts of work, from mending saucepans to making gates and railings and creating candlesticks and other pieces for churches – I did a big crucifix for the spire of a church at Brentwood for a local architect.

A fair amount of tourists come in and start chatting about the work. It's quite nice to show the old place to people. There aren't many town forges left now.

I try to set aside a little time each year to do some of my own work. Some while back I made a large dragonfly, an 8ft little beastie which was quite fun to do. It's on the wall of my house in Sun Street at the moment.

I seem to be pretty busy. There's been quite a revival in metal work, with an emphasis on the contemporary, although you have to cater for old-fashioned tastes, too. People regularly ask me to make things for their homes: I've currently got commissions for five or six curtain rails in Lewes.

Ben Autie has retained an earlier blacksmith's sign above his door. Parts of the forge date from Georgian times.

Swanborough Nurseries

Lydia Collison has run her greengrocer's shop in Fisher Street for the last twenty-four years.

I've survived here by working hard, and by offering fresh fruit and vegetables – some from Brighton market and some from local growers. My brother gets up at 2 o'clock every morning. We do quite a bit of delivering, to Nevill, Landport and Iford, and he looks after that, too.

We don't do fancy stuff, unless people order it. Our passing trade is very local. The High Street's got much quieter at the top, and the farmers' market affects us a lot. It's only one Saturday a month, but that makes a hell of a lot of difference to a little shop like us.

Oh no, you certainly can't take a picture of me! Take a photograph of the shop.

6 Pells

Colin Richards

A retired chartered accountant, Colin Richards moved to Lewes from London in 1985. His chief recreational interests are music and the visual arts.

I find Lewes a very good place to live because it's within easy reach of the country and the sea. I don't drive, but Lewes has excellent communications. Getting into Brighton and Eastbourne or down to Seaford is very easy, and it's just over an hour to London. The Pells seems to me a midpoint between town and country, because within ten minutes you can walk up to the high street and be in the middle of Lewes, or you can walk along the river – either to Tesco's, which is usefully close, or in the other direction out towards Offham, Hamsey and Barcombe Mills and a good range of country pubs.

The Pells feels like a village on its own. It's got its church, Ron's stores, the Elephant Castle pub and Lewes New School. It's a real mix from birth to death – from families with young babies to the churchyard of St John sub Castro which overlooks my house and which has a wildlife area with great views of the Downs all the way round.

It's a great area for the arts. I've a sculptor living next door, and one of her works is always displayed in the front garden. We've got Lewes Little Theatre along Lancaster Street, which puts on a whole range of productions, and the church is a great focal point for concerts, which they put on all through the year. I've heard Vivaldi and Purcell performed recently, for instance, and Emma Kirkby sang here last year.

One of the great family things about the Pells is the open air swimming pool, the oldest in the country. It's fantastic for all ages, and it provides a good outlet for the energies of the teenagers in the summer, even though they perhaps go over the wall at night when it's supposed to be closed. It's spring water and lovely to swim in. The pool is completely surrounded by trees, and there's a park next door, with play equipment for small children.

A few years ago the local council allowed the pool to run down, but since the community group took it over it's been fantastic. I've got a season ticket.

Lewes New School

Adrienne Campbell is the administrator (and a founder-parent) of Lewes New School, which is part of the Human Scale Education movement. The school opened in 2000 in the building of the former Pells primary school.

We're a reluctant private school, because we believe that what we offer should be available to everyone. We believe that, in school, children should be allowed to be themselves, with a chance to have fun, be creative and learn real skills.

You could say that we're slightly alternative, and might therefore seem to be typically Lewes. In fact, however, there's a left-wing philosophy common in Lewes which is against private education, so I'm afraid that we don't get the full cross-section of local people. My view is that some parents are putting their philosophy before their children.

We've decided to have a school for sixty children in the main school and twenty in the kindergarten, and we're almost full now. We have small classes of up to twenty children, with a spread of two years or so in each class. We're less authoritative than mainstream schools. We're against a fear-based rewards/punishment educational culture, and the children call us by our first names. We're not permissive, though. We do have a structure and boundaries – for example, we teach maths and English most mornings, but most of our work is based on topics, and we do try to accommodate children who learn in different ways, such as through their bodies or hearing.

The children are here until the age of eleven, and in terms of private education elsewhere we're very cheap – the fees are about £3,500 a year. This is a delightful community of adults and children finding new ways of learning together.

Kindergarten children on their way back to school along Pelham Terrace after an outing at the Pells.

Pells Pool

Ricardo Magee is manager of the Pells Pool, which is claimed to be the oldest and largest outdoor swimming pool in the country, and whose slogan is 'run by the community for the community'.

I've been here since the middle of May. The previous manager was here for two years, and that's when the Pells Pool Community Association took over from the council. It's a registered charity, run entirely by itself, with some funding from the council and other donors.

With the help of the weather this has been the most successful season so far. People come from all over East Sussex and beyond – it's really quite famous now.

People say the water's very cold here. It is at the beginning of the season, but because it's been so hot this year the water temperature's actually been up to 25 degrees and more. If it still feels cold, that's because of the air temperature – on a hot day I think it's really beautiful in there. The water's fed by a natural spring, and we top the pool up most days. It comes in very cold then, so there are particular times of day when it's best not to come – and it's a lot colder on the bottom left-hand side of the pool, the shallow end, than the other.

I'm very experienced working in swimming pools, but this is very different from the rest. It's intense – incredibly busy. I've never seen anything like it. On sunny days, when we open at 12 o'clock, the queue's all the way up the hill. We should be fine for another season next year. The plan is that, after that, the lottery grant that's going to help rejuvenate the Pells area, both the lake system and the pool, will allow us to make some big improvements.

Pippa Burley

Sculptor Pippa Burley is Colin's next door neighbour.

This is the fifth year we've opened the house for Artwave. It's just for two weekends. I spend so much time alone in my Brighton studio that it's good to get feedback on what I do, even if it can be a bit exhausting meeting so many people all at once.

I work entirely in clay, and I've begun to use local Lewes people as models – they can buy the sculptures if they wish, but that's not the point of it.

How would I describe my work? Well, I try to draw out the spiritual aspect of people – but if that sounds at all pretentious please cut it out!

Pippa Burley with one of her sculptures.

House for sale; art for viewing.

The Elephant & Castle pub.

The church of St John sub Castro.

Lewes Little Theatre

Joyce Fisher is artistic director of Lewes Theatre Club. A former teacher of English and Communication Studies, she also both acts and directs in Lewes Little Theatre productions. Her husband John is an artist, and has created many set designs for the club.

Drama's always been my passion. I took on this job a year after I retired. I wouldn't have been able to do it while I was working, because it's very involving. It's a lot of hassle, and if anything goes wrong the buck stops with me, but it's difficult to explain the excitement of live theatre if you don't have it.

The club was formed in 1939, and a home was found for the existing Lewes Players in a redundant Baptist chapel – the building we have now, although there have been many additions since, including a balcony, foyers, dressing rooms and a bar. The first full length play was J.B. Priestley's *I Have Been Here Before* in 1941 – plays during the war were partly performed for the troops who were stationed around here. Early this year we put that play on again, and our President, John Cull, who lit it the first time, when he must have been extremely young, lit it again. He did have someone helping him!

It costs only £5 a year to join, and £3 if you're retired. It hasn't changed for many years, but we want to keep it low so that it's easy for people to join. Our membership is currently 1900. If they all wanted to come to every show in our 158-seat auditorium they of course wouldn't get in, but they pick and choose. There are occasions when it's hard to get tickets, and we do have very high attendances – an 80 to 90 per cent average for the season, which most theatres would cry for. We're a theatre club, so you have to join in order to buy a ticket. This is a bit of a nuisance, in that we can't sell tickets to the general public, but we do get a lot of financial concessions because we're a private club. We're also a charity, and our aims commit us to putting on quality theatre and taking an educational attitude to the enjoyment of it.

Theatre's a bit like a microcosm of society, because you need so many talents, backstage, onstage, front of house, admin, computer people and so on. It's very largely staffed by retired people, and this is a problem we're addressing – we must renew the membership at the bottom end, and we're having some success with this.

We've a very popular and flourishing youth theatre on Tuesday evenings, which has a waiting list. The youth leader, Pip Henderson, is the only person we pay, if not very much, because we think we need a professional. They do a show of their own devising once a year which is great fun.

Joyce Fisher as a clown in Lewes Theatre Club's production of The Resistible Rise of Arturo Ui by Bertolt Brecht in November 2002. Keith Willoughby is the other clown with (left to right) Nicola Bloom, Lyndsey Meer and Mark Gourley.

7 Wallands

Marietta van Dyck

Marietta is a freelance artist and illustrator who has lived in Lewes for thirteen years. She is the author of Hidden Lewes – an artist's eye for detail.

The Wallands is a very pleasant area, with lovely tree-lined streets such as de Warrenne Road and Prince Edward's Road, which runs right through the estate from the Offham Road to Nevill Road. Certainly my home in Ferrers Road is the quietest place that I've ever lived. It was simply a downland track in the 1920s, and it developed piecemeal as people from Gundreda Road sold off the ends of their gardens. A lot of academics live in the Wallands, because there's a good choice of rather large, relatively secluded houses. The streets are all named after people who arrived with the Norman Conquest or were connected with the Battle of Lewes in 1264.

I like Lewes very much. I've moved about a lot, and I've always chosen to try and live in a smallish market town where, if you get deeply involved with things as I am (the Friends of Lewes, *Lewes News*, the church and so on), you feel that what you do does have some impact. I'd have been lost in a huge conurbation like Brighton and Hove. In Lewes there's plenty going on, and from my point of view, artistically – as I specialise in the drawing of ancient buildings – it's a wonderful place to live and a constant inspiration to me.

Although there are a lot of detached houses here, people do get to know each other to a certain extent, and Christ Church – the local United Reformed and Methodist church – helps to provide a sense of identity. The Congregational church, as it was then, moved up here from Cliffe (where Superdrug is now) after the building was compulsorily purchased for development. I imagine that they got this funny little triangular patch of land pretty cheap, because it

The redeveloped Christ Church.

Marietta in front of the Christ Church tapestry.

was on steep ground, with difficult access from the road. It had only six members at that stage, so to build a new church was a great act of faith. We have about eighty members now, and we've just completed a £600,000 redevelopment scheme with some extremely generous grants, including one from the United Reformed Church's Southern Province – which is the only one with any money! – so we've got just £80,000 to find ourselves.

We have a service every Sunday morning and an evening service twice a month, and we do attract a fair number of young people. Drawing in the local community is a particular emphasis. It's a joke that you get the best food at social dos at the United Reformed Church. There's a friendship lunch on the second Friday of each month (you get a very good meal for £1.50) and there's plenty of room to sit and talk.

Something else that happens here is the folding and collating of the *Lewes News*. I used our splendid new kitchen recently to make tea and coffee for the team in the church hall. What we're rather hoping is that people who get married at the church will now choose to use our church hall for their reception.

In 1996 Iris Smith and I began making the Christ Church Embroidery, which covers 100,000 square centimetres and now hangs inside the church. Several women

from the church also contributed pieces. The overall idea was a fanciful semi-bird's-eye view from the Downs north of Lewes with a shepherd at the centre. Iris produced the bold elements of the design, while I delight in detail: she later died, and I miss her very much. While the church was being renovated the Pells School at Landport looked after it for us for a whole year. They had it in their gym, and the children were delighted. I understand that they're going to try to do something similar, but in paper collage.

Our Wallands primary school has a good reputation. I imagine that it was built in the '50s, but it's in what one might loosely call an Art Deco style. You see a lot of schools and technical colleges in the whole of the south-east of England built in that style. They've got a sort of rounded end, which is perhaps a staircase, and very much a horizontal emphasis to the building. I see a lot of the children going up and down my road. And in King Henry's Road there's the junior section of Lewes Old Grammar School.

Before I came here Wallands had two shops. One was near the bottom of de Warenne road. You'll see two large wooden gates, and there was a shop in there in what I think was originally a stable block. That's long gone, but the corner store at the bottom of Leicester Road is very popular. They're very friendly and helpful people. I don't do my whole weekly shop there, but I'm in and out regularly, and they always know who I am.

Leafy Prince Edward's Road.

Edward VII letter box in Park Road, a drawing by Marietta van Dyck.

Looking down Leicester Road from Prince Edward's Road, with one of the ornamental lamp standards in the foreground.

Lewes News

Fran Whittle was one of the founders of the Lewes News, *which was first published in 1979 and is run entirely by volunteers. For many years a community worker in Lewes, she was involved in the development of the All Saints Arts and Youth Centre, and is now the national and international coordinator of WWOOF (UK and Independents) World Wide Opportunities on Organic Farms. She lives in Bradford Road*

As with many many ideas in Lewes, several people were thinking about starting a community-run newspaper, and it just came together. Paul Hathaway worked for Social Services as a local community officer, Julian Seymour was a local teacher, Pauline Tear was producing a news sheet for the local women's group and David Hurford worked at the YMCA.

At that time a lot of people weren't happy with the *Sussex Express*. We were all aware that there was a need for the community to be able to write accurately about its activities, sometimes at length, and to talk to each other through writing. We wanted people to write their own material, and if they felt they couldn't do that we would help them – but essentially we didn't want to be cutting and editing people's articles.

I was very anxious, and still am, that the paper shouldn't be taken over by any one group. I was born in New Road and moved to Landport when I was eight. As one of the few children who went to the grammar school, I became aware of how class-divided Lewes was and how hard it was for some people to have a voice. When I was

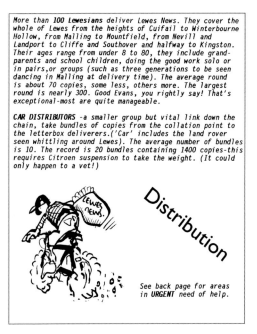

More than **100 Lewesians** deliver Lewes News. They cover the whole of Lewes from the heights of Cuifail to Winterbourne Hollow, from Malling to Mountfield, from Nevill and Landport to Cliffe and Southover and halfway to Kingston. Their ages range from under 8 to 80, they include grandparents and school children, doing the good work solo or in pairs,or groups (such as three generations to be seen dancing in Malling at delivery time). The average round is about 70 copies, some less, others more. The largest round is nearly 300. Good Evans, you rightly say! That's exceptional-most are quite manageable.

CAR DISTRIBUTORS -a smaller group but vital link down the chain, take bundles of copies from the collation point to the letterbox deliverers.('Car' includes the land rover seen whittling around Lewes). The average number of bundles is 10. The record is 20 bundles containing 1400 copies-this requires Citroen suspension to take the weight. (It could only happen to a vet!)

Distribution

See back page for areas in **URGENT** need of help.

LEWES NEWS was first issued in October 1979. It was the idea of a small group of people, shortly supported by a very well attended meeting at the All Saints Centre. The policy is to have a paper which the community writes itself so that people can express opinions, ask questions, inform others about activities, record the past, document the present, wonder about the future-hopefully to bring about greater understanding. In this way the community can talk to, and about itself.

If you still have specific questions which have not been answered, **please** write to 17, Bradford Road,Lewes.

Policy & History

(Cartoons by Raphael Whittle)

in a position to do so, I wanted to make sure that all sections of Lewes society had the opportunity to be involved in *Lewes News*.

That's still the philosophy twenty-four years on. We believe that this *is* the community's paper. We actively encourage people to participate. Different groups are invited to take the supplements or the middle pages, which give them a considerable amount of space in which to describe their activities or make their points.

If people come up to me in the street and talk about some matter of interest or concern to a wider audience, I always ask them to write it up for *Lewes News*. If they write too much I'll get back to them and ask them to cut it, or I might suggest that they wait for the next issue where there might be more space, but I very rarely rewrite. We've had letters from people saying that the level of English used is 'absolutely disgusting' and that the writer doesn't know this or that grammatical law. To that we'd say 'Come and work with us; see how we approach the paper'. People have different ways of talking and writing. We only want to make sure that people are getting their message across: the 'voice' should be theirs. Mr Whittington, for instance, who used to run a newsagent's shop by the Black Horse, wrote, for many years, a series of stories about his life in Lewes from early boyhood. He had a unique way of 'talking' on paper, and I wouldn't have dreamed of losing that flavour or content.

Changes in technology have brought both benefits and problems. I'm computer literate myself, but I've resisted totally changing over to a computer-generated setting-up process. I think it leaves many people behind, people who don't even have access to a typewriter – we still receive a huge amount of hand-written copy. There's a satisfaction in handling all these pieces and eventually getting it all pasted up on to the sheets: you need to like doing jigsaw puzzles. I want to keep as many people as possible involved in all the processes of production even if it isn't the most technologically advanced method.

There are more than 300 people regularly involved, and some of them have been there for every issue since 1979. Paste-up is done on my kitchen table but it is, and has been, moveable. Collating and folding now takes place in Christ Church's hall, but that operation, too, has been in many venues around the town. People often ask why we don't have that done mechanically. Well, apart from the extra cost, it's a great social occasion!

As to the costs, our sponsors and advertisers support the paper even though we never want to have more than a quarter of it as advertisements. We've only ever had enough money in hand for the next issue, but that's fine.

I hope the system doesn't change too much in the future. It's not my paper and I've always made that clear. As coordinator, I of course put in a huge amount of work, and I really care about it, but so do many others – which is why it's still an important feature of this community.

Leicester Road Stores

Rajesh Patel, born in Kenya, came to Lewes from India more than twenty years ago when he was ten years old, attended Priory School and was until recently a regular performer for Lewes Priory cricket club. His sister Nalini runs the stores in Landport (see page 27) with her husband Naresh. Rajesh took over the Leicester Road store from his father.

When my father bought the shop it had a bad name, and it took us about ten years to build it up. It carried only two or three of each item in the shop. We built it up by introducing an off-licence and selling newspapers, and by making sure that we stocked what the customers wanted. If I get a special request I'm very happy to go and find what it is they're after. At Christmas time in particular I'll be hunting down special things people want. People say we're a friendly shop. The fact is that I've been in Lewes a long time and I've got to know a lot of people.

Rajesh and Pinal Patel with their regional award for 'first class standards and merchandising techniques'.

I start at 4.30 in the morning and work through until 7 in the evening, but I do get a few hours' break around lunchtime. People come in early for their papers. It's a good place to work. Leicester Road is in a conservation area – have you noticed the lamps in the street? They're the more traditional type. We get people from the Prince Edward's Road area and from the flats along the way.

We deliver quite a lot of papers. Two shops on the High Street closed, and that's given us more trade. It's a family business, and we do pride ourselves on a good service. That's why I get happiness out of it. Yes, I enjoy it. Working about ninety hours a week wouldn't be easy otherwise, but the time goes quicker than a normal day's work.

There are a lot of old people here. My father was so good at looking after them, and I think I've taken that over from him. Sometimes they'll stop to tell me what's troubling them, and I like to listen if I'm not too busy. We also deliver groceries for a few of the older people who can't carry things easily. That's not an official service, but we know who needs it and it's the kind of thing we like to do.

8 Market Street

Lally Freeborn

Lally is a health visitor, a town councillor, mother to Liam, Alfie and Millie and partner to Nigel, author and historian.

This street has a real buzz. It begins by the war memorial, between the Crown Inn and Fox's estate agents, so there are always people thronging about. Saturday morning in particular is lovely. You come out of the front door and all the tourists are going by – in fact sometimes it's hard to keep them out of the house, because they seem to think it's another shop. Perhaps that's because we live next door to the flea market, where people are always coming and going. And there's Fillers, the sandwich bar, which always seems to have a queue spilling out of the door.

Lally with daughter Millie on the threshold of her house.

I like the smells, too. There's the Italian restaurant which until recently was called Il Patio, and is now Lazzati's. They send a lovely smell of garlic into the air, which drifts into the garden. On the other side of us (in fact, right next door) is George Justice, a place which takes you back fifty years. Colin and his son Jonathan are always shuffling in and out in their lovely big leather aprons, carrying beautiful bits of ancient upholstery, and you can smell the wood whenever you open the door. Occasionally they'll have bags of left-over shavings which we grab and use for the reptiles downstairs: we keep snakes.

We all know each other along here. Colin celebrated fifty years with the firm by throwing an all-day party, with people from all the long-established businesses in the town. Just across the road there's John Stockdale, with his old shop front window and his two Jack Russell dogs – people are always staring in at them barking madly and dashing around. He produces CDs for plant experts, that's his business, and he's also the voice of the Labour Party in Lewes.

He's rather proud of the black mathematical tiles on the front of his house. Quite a few houses along here have them.

Trudi at the Pine Chest is a cheerful presence – she's often outside sweeping the pavement. Her husband Sluff is a musician, and he enjoys giving you a profound comment on the world's politics. Then there's the architect Mike Helps, who's also an ornithologist. That's very useful, because the flea market, which is an old chapel, has a colony of swifts each year, and every so often the babies fall down and I don't know what to do with them. Mike will come along and we usually end up putting them in the guttering at the top – they either make it or they don't!

Remembrance Sunday's always busy at the war memorial, and the Crown is the home of Waterloo bonfire society, so 5 November is a noisy occasion. I love all that – until midnight, at least – but I'm not so keen on the traffic which charges down the street. It's a bit of a pain. When we had the fuel shortage a few years ago it was lovely, because the road was a lot quieter for a time. Those railings you see along the pavement used not to exist. What happened was that a huge lorry came thundering down and went into Marion's house – right into her sitting room, in fact. She occasionally helps Trudi out in the Pine Chest.

Fillers

Tina Carroll opened the Fillers sandwich bar three years ago.

I'm here at 6 o'clock every morning, and I'll serve anyone who comes in that early. I work through until 3. We get through twenty-five brown loaves and fourteen white loaves every day – and each loaf makes eight sandwiches. We do get asked for some unusual combinations sometimes, such as egg mayo and prawn and honey and banana. The worst thing I've ever been asked for was banana and stilton toasties. It wasn't very nice doing that.

The view down Market Street from the war memorial.

The painting of Thomas Paine in the Market Tower by local artist Julian Bell. He has also painted several inn signs in Lewes, including the Lamb in Fisher Street and the Swan in Southover.

Flea Market

Alan Wilkinson ran flea markets in Newhaven and Brighton before opening the one in Market Street eight years ago.

The term 'flea market' indicates that we sell a complete mixture of things – antiques, books, junk, if you like. I think there's an English disease that we like secondhand shops and poking around looking for a bargain, but we do get a lot of dealers and tourists, too. Lewes is a good town for us, partly because of the tourists, which helps, but also because it has a couple of popular auction rooms.

There are quite a few antiques shops in the town. They're a bit posher than we are. We do a bit of everything, and I personally think that helps us. They're restricted by doing only antiques, and the trade has changed. There's a trend towards more modern things in this country, although we might just be going through a phase. I don't think the antiques business is what it was.

Our price range? Cheapest 20 pence I should think, or even less, to pieces of furniture for £300 or £400 – occasionally for over £1,000, but not very often. We let the space out to about sixty stallholders. They buy their stuff from all sorts of places: auction rooms, private houses, boot fairs. They leave it priced up, but we run the place and take the money. With some street markets they have to stand behind their stall, but we do it all for them. Some of them are more serious than others. I'd suggest that for about a half it's almost a social thing – a hobby – but even the others probably don't do it for a complete living. They're retired, or have another job.

Getting a bargain is more difficult these days because more people are at it. If you watch the TV programmes, you'll know that it's harder to find something for a fiver that's worth £10,000. That doesn't happen. But all the time you see people going to boot fairs and buying things for a pound or two which here, in a retail situation, they might be able to sell for five or ten. If they do a few of those a week it's worth having the stall, and it's a bit of fun. I've heard that there have been some coups here – certainly a couple of cheapish pictures that have been bought here and have ended up down at Gorringe's for a few hundred pounds more than they were bought for.

The Pine Chest

Trudi Lindon and Godfrey (Sluff) Hazell opened their Pine Chest shop twenty-three years ago. Trudi meets the customers, while Sluff and his son Philip make many of the pine beds, book cases, coffee tables and shelf units. Trudi, a German, used to teach the language at Lewes Prison.

I did that for more than twenty years – I'd see people coming in for their second sentence – but I gave it up soon after we started the business. It's a full-time job. We sell wooden toys, lamp shades and other accessories apart from the furniture. Most of it's made in this country, but the reclaimed timber furniture comes from Poland.

There's been a decline in the number of shops in the area since we've been here, as you can tell by the number of private houses with large windows. We had a

butcher's next door at one time, and most of the businesses have either closed or changed. I think we're reaching a critical level now, because you need a good number of small individual shops in order to attract people to the town.

Fortunately for us we've the North Street car parks below us. We're in a prominent position for people walking up the hill to the High Street.

Trudi and Sluff outside their shop. Sluff plays baritone and alto saxophone for the trad jazz Society Syncopators and is a regular in the Expedient Band which forms part of the bonfire procession each 5 November.

George Justice

Colin Tompsett began working for his uncle at George Justice's in 1952 and took over the business with a partner in 1963. He now runs it with his son Jonathan.

George Justice founded the firm in 1910, and I think a great deal of his work was for the American art collector Edward Perry Warren – the man who brought Rodin's *The Kiss* to Lewes. I took the business over at a very bad time for Lewes, because buildings were being pulled down all over the place for a proposed inner relief road. Our workshop and the two cottages on either side of us were going to be demolished to make way for a car park, and for ten years we were alone here, with unoccupied buildings on either side. Then there was a change of plan and at last the street came to life again.

Colin Tompsett (left) and his son Jonathan in their workshop.

I started in joinery, but I was always more inclined to cabinet making. In the 1950s and '60s the sculptor John Skelton used to design church furnishings and we'd make most of the pieces for him. We used to make all sorts of special pieces for all manner of people, mainly of oak but of mahogany, too.

There's not so much call for original pieces today. People go for the mass-produced stuff, which of course is usually much cheaper. We're mainly restorers now, although we do some cabinet making and french polishing. We take in every type of furniture – chairs, tables, chests of drawers, bureaux – from the earliest pieces in oak to modern items. We've a good collection of before-and-after photographs, showing how complete wrecks can be transformed.

People come to us from a 50-mile radius, and some of our customers are the third generation of their family to use us. A lot of our work comes from recommendations.

Cobblers

Graham Taylor served a seven-year apprenticeship in Northampton as a shoe-maker and shoe-repairer before opening his cobbler's business in Market Street thirty years ago.

Nowadays people don't know the difference between a cobbler's and a heel bar. Most men in the street could do what a heel bar does. I'm a trained cordwainer. I supply the entire company of Glyndebourne – they don't go anywhere else. I sell Northampton shoes which are bench-made by craftsmen. I hand-sew. I don't just do repairs for people in Lewes. People come to me from London, the north and abroad. Riding boots are sent to me from all over England.

I started off making shoes, working in the clicking room – the knife you run across the leather makes a clicking sound – and went on through as an inkboy, inking up shoes. When I learnt it, all the heels on a ladies' shoe were stack leather or wood, but nowadays 90 per cent of them are plastic, no matter the price. I do them in here from thirty bob to six hundred to thousands, but still plastic heels.

People think I'm out the back just banging on rubber heels, but I do all types of leather work – bag repairs, suitcases, gun cases. People are crying out for tradesmen, but they can't get them. People come for miles to have a zip put in, and they'll pay anything from £25 to £100, depending on the job. Two years ago a man came in here, who was going on tour in Ireland. He wanted a bandolier made, and I said 'What for?' He had ten harmonicas that all played a different tune, and there had to be a different pocket for each one with a little pop-over flap. That came to over £150 and he jumped at it.

I'm a falconer. I breed falcons and hawks, and that's my passion. It's the oldest field sport in the world, going back thousands of years, and not much has changed. We still use leather jessies and hoods. You can buy a hood for about £75. They're beautiful, and some people don't use them – they like to collect them. I make my own, because you lose them and fall on them and crush them when you're running across the field after your falcon. Ha, ha!

9 Nevill

Luke Rideout

Luke (aged ten) lives with his five-year-old brother Joe and his parents, Paul and Sarah, in East Way.

I've lived in East Way all my life, and the Nevill estate is great if you like being in the outdoors as I do. We've got the Downs very close, so we go up and have a climb about there, and it's good for cycling. We don't go up by ourselves because there are chalkpits, and it can be quite dangerous. I've got lots of my friends close by – Emrys, Kristian, Andrew and Matthew, who all go to Western Road School with me, although a lot of the Nevill children go to Wallands, which is a bit closer.

There are lots of places to play apart from the Downs. Sometimes we go down to the green by the main road, which is two minutes' away and where there are swings and a nice big field for football. Every year we have Nevill Sports Day there. There are races for all the children on the estate, including sack races, obstacle races and egg and spoon races. The estate roads aren't very busy, so you can play outside if you're careful – although my mum says the cars go too fast and that there should be a 20-miles-an-hour speed restriction. We've got two local shops, and I go to one of them for sweets and for my weekly comic, which is the *Beano*. We get things like milk, bread and cheese from the other one.

Up at the top, near the Downs, there are allotments. Some have been there a long time, but we've got one which is part of the Lewes organic allotments project. There are six plots up there, and a wildlife area f or children. My friends and I sometimes go up and help. At first it was all overgrown by cow parsley, and we started hacking that away. That was just for fun, but then we thought it would be a good idea to have an allotment of our own. My dad helped by strimming it. We planted everything, and it looked perfectly fine, but when we came back later all the weeds had shot up. The potatoes had started growing as well, but something had been at the onions. We had sunflowers, too.

Luke with some of his stick insects.

I go to a club called Woodcraft, which is based in a hall on the other side of the main road – St Mary's Hall in Christie Road. It's fun. It's not what you think – not about woodcraft, but hiking and other things. We do tent-making, science projects and cookery. We've made cakes, banoffee pie and pizzas. There's plenty to do on the estate. There's even a bonfire society especially for children.

Every year there's a thing called Nevill in Bloom, when gardens open all over the estate and you can go inside and have a look at them. That's where I got my stick insects. They were very cheap – three for £1 – so I got six of them for £2. They haven't bred yet, but let's hope they do. If they manage it we'll get a bigger container – I think they'll deserve one. I certainly won't sell them, because I like keeping

Luke and brother Joe on their allotment.

them. First of all their front legs go red by the joints, and then the middle legs go yellow. I think the back legs are going to go blue. My biggest one is about 10cm long at the moment. They grow to up to half a metre – yes, really! They'll grow huge.

The Green is a great facility for the youngsters of the Nevill estate.

Mount Harry Stores

The Dhesi family have lived on the Nevill estate for fifteen years. Apinder Dhesi has been running the Mount Harry Stores with her husband Des for the past ten years, and before this the shop was run by Des's brother and his wife.

It's good to live in the same community as many of our customers. This is a friendly estate, and we have a lot of good regulars. We sell a large range of general groceries, as well as a large, well-stocked off-licence, half-price national newspapers and my own, home-made Punjabi food in the chill cabinet. That goes very well.

Over the years we've had to adapt the shop to fit in with changing demands. We used to close on Sundays, but when the supermarkets started opening every day we had to follow suit – now we open from seven in the morning until nine in the evening every day of the week. This is a family business, so we don't employ any staff. We have a large family, and everybody mucks in to help out.

My two children went to the local schools here. We live just a few doors away from the shop and have many friends and good neighbours. We were in south London before coming to Lewes, and we all agree that moving here, and becoming part of such a close-knit community, is the best thing we ever did. Our customers are loyal to us and very supportive, and our children have grown up together.

Nevill Newsagents

It's less than a year since Sigi Danklmayer, an Austrian, took over the newsagents with his Chinese wife Xiomu.

I had a business in London for many years, and I can tell you that I've never worked in a nicer place than this. Eighty per cent of my customers are on first-name terms. We employ local staff, and we sell local milk and eggs.

We have six morning newspaper rounds, two in the evenings and four on Sundays, chiefly covering the Nevill estate. We deliver about 260 papers a day, quite apart from those that are ordered but collected from the shop and others that are sold over the counter. The *Mail*, *Telegraph* and *Sun* are the best sellers, in that order, but we get a good demand for the *Sussex Express*, too.

Making a living as a corner shop isn't difficult if you give a service. It was in response to our customers' demands, for instance, that we started our off-licence – not in order to attack the shop next door, although that's what they seem to think. I understand that there's a history of ill-feeling between the two shops, and that some people will always go in one rather than the other, but I'd rather that wasn't the case. They've cut the price of newspapers to annoy us, but it doesn't. I believe that competition is healthy. If you had one store instead of two there'd be a monopoly and that wouldn't be good for the local people.

I can see that you find this situation amusing – and I think you're probably right!

The Nevill estate has two shops cheek by jowl – and competition is fierce.

Nevill Juvenile Bonfire Society

Mike Fisk is secretary, and a former chairman, of Nevill Juvenile Bonfire Society, founded in the late 1960s.

We operate in the same way as the five major Lewes bonfire societies, and we sometimes march with Cliffe on 5 November, but we have our procession and fire on a Saturday around a week before the main event. It's at the site the Borough uses. We have tableaux and effigies, and even an archbishop – although he's an adult rather than one of the youngsters.

There are about 350 members, and half of them are children. Although we welcome members from outside, it's very much an estate thing. Preparations go on for months in advance, and the young people get a lot out of it.

South Street used to be a juvenile society, but a few years ago they dropped that title. We're probably the only juvenile bonfire society in the world!

10 School Hill

Winnie Pallen

Winnie came to Lewes from London almost sixty years ago, after being evacuated with her baby daughter Annette during the second world war. The family moved to her present home in School Hill after a short spell in Landport. Her husband Albert died six years ago.

So many of the shops have changed during my time here. Downstairs there's been an electrician, a furrier, some French photographers (very nice people – they wanted to adopt Annette!), a shop selling lampshades and others I can't immediately think of. Mr Bannerman, who later owned the Gourmet down the road on the other side, had a coffee shop here before it became Tizz's.

There was a cinema across the road where the *Sussex Express* is. The De Luxe. They had a little sweet shop that belonged to it, called the Chocolate Box. I've been to that cinema with an umbrella up, because it used to leak upstairs. And if you had any sweets and you put your hand down while you were watching a film a little mouse would come up. But they used to have beautiful films.

I remember when there was a dairy a few doors up, where the Liberal Democrats are now. The woman who owned it married Mr Yates who ran the chemist's where Prickly Pear now is, and she closed it in order to join him.

The Emporium antiques place over the road used to be Hammonds, selling curtains, and the hairdresser's was Coutt's, the menswear shop. Further down there was a little shoe shop, and during the war a tank went into it. Not many people remember this, but towards the end of the war German prisoners used to sweep the roads here.

School Hill was even busier than it is now before the Cuilfail tunnel was built. It's central here, and I can sit in the window and watch people go past. I walk down to Safeway for my shopping every day – although coming back up the hill is another cup of tea! I've got plenty of friends, and the neighbours are very good to me. David downstairs – that's Tizz – is a lovely boy (I'm old enough to be able to call him darling!), and he'll do things for me. He's put a little security light and camera in the passageway. There's a lovely family next door, too. I love living here.

Octave Recorded Music Specialists

Andy How was a professional photographer when, fifteen years ago, he visited the record shop in School Hill, told the owner that it was the kind of place he'd like to own and was immediately invited to make an offer.

When we took over it was about 70 per cent vinyl and tapes, but it's changed over the years until it's now 100 per cent CD with a much greater emphasis on classical music and specialist material. Lewes is an artistic town and the people have many different musical tastes. The proximity to Glyndebourne has an influence, too.

They like blues, jazz, imported reissued rock – anything that you would expect to go into a shop and have someone help you find rather than the attitude of 'Well, if it's not on the shelf we haven't got it'. We're not often defeated. Over the years I've developed an enormous amount of sources, so I can track down most things.

Steamer Trading

Steamer Trading was founded in Alfriston in 1985 by Lizzie Phillips, former home editor of the Sunday Times, *and her husband David, the first buying director of Habitat. The company now has cook shops in Lewes, Brighton, Eastbourne, Battle and Heathfield as well as its original Alfriston store, and has won several prestigious awards. Ben Phillips, managing director (and son of the founders), says Lewes was the obvious place to begin the expansion.*

Lewes was a place we'd lived alongside and always loved. Whenever you come to it you can't fail to be startled by its architecture and its diversity – it's a stunning town, one of the most beautiful in the country, and there's so much that captures your imagination. Our first shop here was in the Riverside Centre, and it was absolutely tiny. One day we spotted this building, which at the time was virtually empty. Originally it was a Victorian ladies' milliners, which gave it that wonderful shopfront, but it had had many different uses over the years and it was in a fairly sorry state. We fully restored it (the Friends of Lewes were kind enough to give us a commendation for that) and it now has a frontage as it used to be, so that people can walk into the front of the shop and there's the wonderful original vitrine – a superb showpiece.

We also put a coffee shop into the store. The original idea was that people would be able to sit down and relax, with somewhere to put the children while they browsed and somewhere to put bored husbands – or bored wives, these days, often as not – but the coffee shop has taken on a life of its own. It's been a huge success and is very important to the nature of the shop, bringing people in at what might otherwise be quiet times.

Everything we stock first has to pass the test of being practical and the best of its class. We cover everything that fits into the kitchen, from pots and pans to coffee machines and decorative china like Emma Bridgewater's hand-decorated English designs. For most people the kitchen is probably the heart of the home, and we supply anything that will make that room special and individual. We watch the major department stores and other retailers very carefully to make sure that we're competitive: Lewes people will be supportive of you, but they very much want to feel at the same time that you're giving a lot back to them, and that they can't get a better service, a better price or a better selection somewhere else.

School Hill has improved dramatically for shopping. A few years ago we would have been stuck among a lot of estate agents and solicitors, very much in between the two main shopping parts of Lewes – down in Cliffe High Street and up by the war memorial – with quite a walk between the two. I think it's probably fair to say that School Hill got a slight lift after the floods of 2000. A lot more people have looked for premises further up from the Cliffe because they did suffer very badly and they're understandably a little bit nervous. We have a very good mix now, and the shops are getting smarter and more interesting all the time.

We like being among specialist shops. Supermarkets do a superb job, but people genuinely have an interest in shopping, and if a high street has something to offer they'll still seek it out. Supermarkets aren't masters of all trades. It's up to retailers to offer something different. The nice thing about Lewes is that there's a very broad mix. There aren't many down-market discount type shops, but a really good selection of unique shops run by people who have a passion for what they do.

Sussex Express

John Eccles worked as a journalist in Brighton, Crawley, Surbiton, Cambridge, Australia and Papua New Guinea before joining the Sussex Express *in 1975. He has been here ever since, serving under several editors, and is the paper's chief reporter.*

I was struck by the charm of Lewes the moment I came here in 1975 and I haven't changed my mind since. A magical early sight, which I still love, was the rain twinkling on the old Victorian brick pavements up St Anne's Hill. Outsiders regard it as a 'brown rice' town, with a Clothkits image, but it's much more varied than that. It's a tolerant sort of place, and people from all walks of life rub shoulders very happily – and there are so many different pubs and clubs that it's easy to avoid those you don't particularly get on with.

You're organising this book by areas, but I'd have done it by pubs. There are so many, and they all have their own character. I spend a large amount of my time in them, and it's where I get a lot of my stories. My current favourite is the Brewers Arms in the High Street, but I also enjoy the Lewes Arms, the Gardener's, the Black Horse and quite a few more. Yes, I've been in them all in my time.

I joined the *Express* after being away from England for seven years. Lewes struck me as the sort of town I liked to dream about in exile – a place I barely believed existed in reality. In other words I was very happy to be here.

The *Express* tries to reflect the town. The newspaper has its devotees and its detractors. That's how things should be. At least people read it – and it's been read since 1837. The newspaper is part of the fabric of Lewes. People knock the 'local rag', but where would they be without it? Like a house or a pub or a church, it slowly evolves. Staff change, technology changes, editorial stances modify, but the *Express* trudges metaphorically on. Every week it's there to be read, pondered upon and then placed in the bin. That's the way of things.

Lewes hasn't changed a great deal over the last twenty-eight years. Some think there's more crime, but I believe that's largely because the police are much more

open about giving information than they used to be. That's great for a reporter, but I suppose it does seem to give a worse impression of the town.

Politically there have been notable changes. I thought it was most enjoyable back in the 1970s when the old-guard Labour councillors were active. You had boisterous debates in those days – they'd have a good shout and then retire to the pub. The Tories ran the place for many years; now they're treading water. The Liberal Democrats are in power today. I'm still waiting to see what they can achieve for this lovely old town.

As for the near future, I believe on-street parking is going to create a big stir in Lewes. The tradition here is 'live and let live', and people don't like being forced into following a single pattern of living. A residents' parking scheme is due to start next year, and I forecast fireworks.

Tizz's

David Johnson ('Tizz'), was born and bred in Lewes. After college in London, he went into set design and began making jewellery for actors, later coming home to set up his jewellery shop.

I was in the Needlemakers for about four years, but I moved to School Hill because it's in the middle of Lewes – halfway up and halfway down between Cliffe High Street and the top. It's a thoroughfare, and people stop half way up the hill for a breather.

There are several silversmiths working in Lewes, but they're all individual. Most of them specialise in one-off pieces in gold, silver, platinum and so on, but we concentrate on imported high-volume fashion jewellery, although we do make up about 20 per cent of what we sell ourselves. We import some high-quality sterling silver jewellery from Bangkok and Mexico, but most of our stuff is at the cheap fashion end of the market – 'loseable jewellery'. It comes from Hong Kong and places like that. I travel looking for it, although not as much as I used to because the internet and fax machines make life a lot easier and that saves me air fares.

A lot of our stuff is Fairtrade. We don't advertise the fact, because I don't like making a song and dance about something you should be doing anyway. When I go abroad on buying trips I hate to see American and European businessmen haggling to knock down the prices of things which cost only a few pence in any case. Then they'll go for a slap-up meal which costs far more than the amount they've saved, and they'll boast about how much they're doing for the Third World.

Norman Baker, MP

*Norman Baker became Liberal Democrat MP for Lewes in 1997, ending
123 years of Conservative rule. He lives above the 'shop' with his wife Liz, their
daughter Charlotte and Liz's daughters Sukey and Alice.*

The first crack in Tory rule appeared when the Lib Dems took control of Lewes District Council in 1991, and I was council leader. That was the springboard of what happened subsequently. Lewes is a very sophisticated political town. It's home for people who work in high-level pressure groups, journalists, top civil servants. Many peers of the realm live in the town or just outside, and you've the background of the Battle of Lewes, Tom Paine and so on. For a small town it punches above its weight politically.

The main part of my job as I see it is to deal with constituents. I spend about half my time here and the other half in London – and I might say that the people in Lewes are much more normal than those in Westminster. It's more satisfying down here, especially when the government has a majority of about 160 and the chances of achieving anything on the floor of the Commons are minuscule. You can achieve things behind the scenes with ministers, and you can get things into the national papers and help change government policy that way, but the most satisfying part of the job is someone coming to you with a justifiable grievance and, because you know who to contact or you know the right way in, you can sort the problem out for them and take a load off their mind.

For some reason I have a reputation for asking lots of questions in the House. Someone told me I was thirteenth this session in the number of questions asked, so I don't actually ask the most. It's a curiosity of the parliamentary system that because the government has such a large majority you can't change legislation. The prime minister's got unparalleled powers compared with other western leaders, in terms of making war, signing treaties, appointing people to the Lords and all the royal prerogative powers which he exercises. He has a vast majority in the Commons thanks to a corrupt voting system, he controls the cabinet and he has the whips, so power is skewed far too much towards the executive. Those of us who aren't part of it, but have a duty of holding the goverment to account, must use whatever weapons we have, and the parliamentary question is one of the few that actually works. I hope I've used it effectively on behalf of my constituents and, more widely, to hold the government to account.

Locally, I think the district council has done a pretty good job overall. Its style has changed since I was leader. It's quieter and more workmanlike, perhaps, which isn't necessarily a bad thing. The town council has been maligned over the years and rather unfairly. In my view the membership of the town council has improved. I don't have the same respect for the county council, which in my view is frankly very poor – and to be honest always was, and therefore doesn't completely reflect the political control. The fact is that you've got a county council which is now seeking to become a minimalist authority. As part of that it wants to asset strip, and so buildings are being sold – Pelham House is only one example of that. We've also got the desire to move the headquarters out of Lewes because, I think, the Conservatives aren't happy with it being in a Lib Dem town, which is a nonsense. That will be a challenge, because in employment terms Lewes survives quite well – as Bonn did in West Germany – by being a place where everything is, but for no obvious reason. Historically, of course, it has been a major centre and the county town, but it's been eclipsed in population terms by Brighton and Eastbourne and yet still retains the county council, the police headquarters, the local primary healthcare trust, the prison and so on. It's important to Lewes that it retains a critical mass of white-collar worker in the public sector. We've already lost the fire headquarters to Eastbourne. If we lose the county council other people may ask why they should be here. We

must make sure that the crown court and magistrates' court stay here, and that Lewes remains a key administrative centre.

John's Hairdressers

John Russell has been cutting men's hair in Lewes for thirty years, and he's produced every known style – plus a few not so familiar.

I first started doing haircutting in the '50s. Before that hair was quite long. People will always say that in their day they had it short, but they didn't – it was very long on top but short at the sides, and they'd sweep it back and grease it down. In the '50s people had the Tony Curtis- and Elvis-style haircuts, which again were fairly long and swept back, and then the '60s saw the college boy haircuts – quite short on top and short at the sides, but not shaved. In the '70s people started wearing their hair long again, over the ears and down over the collar. That went on for a good ten years, until it started reverting back again, and you had the skinheads.

Various stars have been in here over the years – the actor Eric Porter, Long John Bawdry – and I've had some interesting challenges, too. I remember one girl who had her hair bleached white, and I had to cut the shape of a tennis ball into it. That looked really good, because it was shaved down to three-sixteenths of an inch. Then there was a coloured gent who wanted a chessboard effect. The hair was black, but when I took it down to the scalp I got a much lighter shade. That was quite interesting.

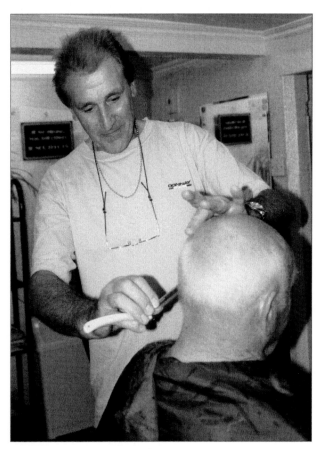

Today the youngsters are having their hair short again, but short all over, with bare clippers right down the sides and the back, graduated in. You have to keep abreast of the names, but once you've worked out what they want it's usually a variation of something you've done years before. I've done a David Beckham – the one where he had it pushed up from the sides to the middle, looking like a Mohican. I've still got a customer who has that done, and he asked for it long before Beckham made it popular. We joke that Beckham got it from him.

I don't shave people any more, although I do put a razor on the back of the neck, which many barbers won't do now. To do it correctly you need lather and soap and hot towels, because the skin is quite tender, but with today's razors people can do it themselves easily enough. Years ago people didn't know how to keep a razor sharp, so they used to go the barber to get shaved. Nobody ever does that now.

I must admit that the short haircuts are the easiest, but the longer ones, where you have to put some shape into the hair and change the style completely, can be much more satisfying if you've got the time to do it.

Seasons Restaurant

Carol Mercer started Seasons thirteen years ago, and is in partnership with her elder daughter, Sophie Hyde. Her younger daughter Andreana runs the shop.

We're vegetarian, vegan and mostly organic, and everything is made on the premises. We also do a lot of outdoor catering – we did Norman Baker's wedding – and we supply Infinity Foods in Brighton. A recent speciality of ours is organic chocolate wedding cakes.

We have regulars who come from quite a long way away, some even from London. I don't mean that they come down solely for lunch, but we're certainly one of the reasons they choose to visit Lewes.

Sophie Hyde at the top of the steps leading down to Seasons.

Lyons Newsagents

Dominic Lyons has run the corner shop at the top of School Hill with his brother Tim for the past twenty years. In his leisure time he's a qualified FA referee and linesman.

I'm up at 4.30 from Monday to Saturday, and I start a quarter of an hour later on Sunday. We're one of a dying breed in Lewes – newsagents who deliver the papers. Our best-selling newspaper is the *Daily Mail*, followed by the *Daily Telegraph*, the *Sun* and the *Argus*. About 70 per cent of our sales are delivered, and that's what distinguishes us from the supermarkets. When they started selling papers, that took the cream off the coffee for us.

The profit margin on newspapers has gone down and down over the years, and we wouldn't survive if we had to pay anyone other than the roundsman. We've no room to expand – and even if we did, the rents would be prohibitive. My fear is what will happen when the council brings in on-street parking next year. People can park for two hours in School Hill at present, and I do wonder whether people will think it worth coming here if they have to pay.

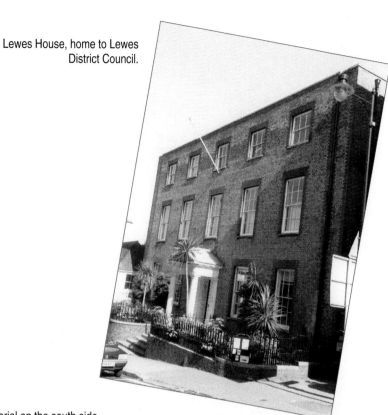

Lewes House, home to Lewes District Council.

Shops immediately below the war memorial on the south side.

11 High Street

John Bleach

John is one of the two senior custodians of Lewes Castle and Barbican House Museum, which are owned by the Sussex Archaeological Society. He was born in Ringmer, and has been with the SAS for more than twenty-six years.

I live in Leicester Road, so to come from home to work and back I'm up and down the High Street at least twice a day, either on foot or on the bike. Every time I approach it in the morning I'm reminded of the fact that Lewes is a linear town. The High Street runs from St Anne's church down to Cliffe bridge, with the twittens and lanes running down steeply to the south, and once you've walked the length of the street you've seen much of historic Lewes.

It's an historic as well as a modern matter of fact that there's no obvious town centre. Many towns organised around a noticeable market-place have a centre which can be focused on in any redevelopment. Perhaps historically the centre would have been this middle area of the High Street from the castle entrance to the top of Station Street where the market would have been, with stalls along the sides of the road. You can still see this in the way the street widens out as you walk down towards Station Street, with the White Hart on your right. You have this wonderful view of Caburn Books, which is almost certainly a medieval encroachment into what was an area of open market space originally. That space probably continued to St Nicholas Lane, and you wouldn't have had the restricted area of today, with the tourist information centre only a handful of yards away from Unicorn Books across the road.

Many of the buildings conceal their age. The Law Courts look early nineteenth century, and that's exactly what most parts of them are, but otherwise the High Street often tends to deceive. I work in Barbican House, and I know it's a timber-framed, late sixteenth-century building. Look at it from the outside and you would have very little idea of this, because at a glance it looks like a Georgian town house. If you stripped away the outside you'd be left with a substantial Elizabethan house. That's one of my enjoyments of living in Lewes, the discovery of the old hidden behind the more recent. And of course when you climb the castle and look down on the roofs, that's very often when you can start seeing the changes – from the ground the older roofs are often hidden behind Georgian developments.

One might regret the fact that the county hall was located next to St Anne's church on a south-facing slope looking down the river valley, which had previously been green, but Lewes managed to escape some of the worst developments of the 1960s and '70s – partly, perhaps, because it's a linear town without a centre to be developed. Another factor is the presence of Brighton just down the road. I suspect that a lot of the development potential was taken up in Brighton, and that's saved Lewes.

You could say that Brighton has also taken trade from Lewes, so that we don't have the larger shops here, but I personally don't mind that. I do nearly all my shopping in Lewes quite happily and it serves most of my needs. If you want to live in a pleasant

historic environment perhaps you have to accept the fact that you won't have large shopping developments. And the High Street appears to have a relatively thriving trading community, with quite a diverse range of goods for people to buy.

Where do I shop in the High Street? I don't use the restaurants myself, but I do occasionally buy things in Beckworths and look into the charity shops. But I'm a book collector, and I'm delighted to say that Lewes is well off for secondhand book shops. As I walk down the street I pass the 15th Century Bookshop; Pipe Passage, with David Jarman's delightful little shop selling books out of his book club; Andrew and Yasmin Cumming; Alan and Jenny Shelley's Bow Windows Bookshop; and now Caburn Books, as well. That's five very good secondhand and antiquarian outlets within a few hundred yards. It's perhaps not on the scale of Hay-on-Wye, but worth the town promoting, I'd have thought.

Lewes Town Hall stands on the site of the Star Inn, where Protestant martyrs were held before being burned at the stake close by.

A plaque on Lewes Town Hall. The Protestant Martyrs are remembered each 5 November, when Lewes mounts the most dramatic bonfire extravaganza in England.

iN THE VAULTS BENEATH THIS BUILDING WERE IMPRISONED TEN OF THE SEVENTEEN PROTESTANT MARTYRS WHO WERE BURNED AT THE STAKE WITHIN A FEW YARDS OF THIS SITE 1555-1557 THEIR NAMES ARE RECORDED ON THE MEMORIAL TO BE SEEN ON CLIFFE HILL

"FAITHFUL UNTO DEATH"

The face of Bacchus, surrounded by grapes and vine leaves, is one of five attractive keystones of the Town Hall façade.

Lewes Tourist Information Centre

Sally Bass is part of Lewes District Council's cultural services department, and runs the Tourist Information Centre in the High Street.

We welcome between 350 and 500 people a day during the summer months. Many have chosen Lewes as a holiday centre, of course, but others have discovered the town by accident, and once they've seen it they're very keen to come again some time in the future.

Although there are fewer American tourists in Britain since 9/11, the more adventurous of them still find their way here, and we get a lot of European visitors, especially from Holland and Belgium. It's the historic aspect that appeals chiefly, plus the town's proximity to so many attractions, including Glyndebourne and the beautiful downland countryside. They also like the fact that we have so many distinctive one-off shops rather than the standard chain stores elsewhere.

If I could add one facility that would add to Lewes's appeal, both for tourists and for local people, it would be a cinema. I sometimes look at the Baxter's printworks, now standing empty in St Nicholas Lane, and think that would be ideal. We get a lot of queries about cinemas, and although Lewes has a thriving film club at the All Saints Centre, people have to go to other towns such as Uckfield and Brighton. An ice rink would be a good idea, too.

It pays to raise your eyes to first-floor level and above when walking about Lewes. This ornate lamp bracket is affixed to H.A. Baker, the chemists.

The Ask restaurant stands on the corner of High Street and Fisher Street.

White Hart Hotel

In 1988 Cliff Ayris returned to England after a year abroad. His family had been in hotels and catering, and now he was looking for a hotel of his own. He finally chose the White Hart, he says, largely because of its location – in a historic county town and close to a host of attractions and the South Downs, to London by rail, to mainland Europe via the ferry and to the rest of the world via Gatwick Airport.

It was a nice, busy little place, but it was much smaller then and had fewer facilities. It was a thirty-bedroom coaching inn. Now it's a fifty-three-bedroom, all en suite, full-service hotel with three function rooms, two lounges, a coffee shop, snack shop,

a full health and fitness suite with indoor swimming pool, gymnasium, sauna, solarium, dance studio and beauty clinic. We've broadened the entire range of facilities so that we can forage into every aspect of the leisure industry.

We like to think of ourselves as a central focal spot for Lewes social life. We touch the local people more as a food and beverage operation than as a hotel, of course, although many do have visitors who stay here. A very large number come through here at least once a year because so many of the clubs and associations use us – tennis, bowls, trout fishing, sailing, the Masons, Rotaries, Round Table, Lions clubs and a lot more.

I don't want to expand my hotel interests anywhere else, because I do very much enjoy this particular establishment and want to make it a lifetime project. Now that the expansion is finished we're concentrating on titivating and refurbishing the hotel – making it a quality product. We have something like 23,000 guest nights each year and 4,000 people a week visiting for various kinds of local trade, so there's a huge throughput here. I want to concentrate on fine-tuning that quality aspect and really giving people a venue that retains their interest. We want them to keep on coming back.

THOMAS PAINE 1737=1809
HERE EXPOUNDED HIS
REVOLUTIONARY POLITICS.
THIS INN IS REGARDED AS
A CRADLE OF AMERICAN
INDEPENDENCE WHICH HE
HELPED TO FOUND WITH
PEN AND SWORD.

Wycherley's

Ivor Wycherley is the great-grandson of the man who founded the family estate agents 150 years ago this year. His son Charles is now responsible for selling and surveying, while his daughter Anne manages the business, but Ivor hasn't stepped back very far.

I'm eighty-one, so I'm down to a five-and-a-half-day week now. What would I do if I wasn't busy? Charles and Anne run their areas, but I do their jobs when they're missing for any reason.

I've of course seen a tremendous rise in prices since I started out in 1938. At that time we were selling houses on the Nevill estate for £675. They're worth

anything from £200,000 to £500,000 today. The most expensive property on our books at the moment has an asking price of £895,000. There's not enough property in Lewes – that's the problem. There's a demand from London commuters and people employed by county hall and the two universities, but practically all the infills have been dealt with now.

If you're buying property as an investment I think the best bargains are down in the Court Road area, close to the magistrates' court. You can get £600 a month for those. I know there's a reluctance to buy properties in the area that was flooded, but I'd take the risk myself. After all, there were forty years between the last two floodings.

The Law Courts.

Carpe Diem sundial.

Beckworths

Rebecca Lane runs Beckworths with her partner Simon Aplin. They both worked in insurance and hated it, so they set up their delicatessen here eight years ago.

You need a theme in order to compete with the supermarkets, and we decided to concentrate on Italian food. We use quite a lot of different suppliers and pick what we like from each one. Lewes people are particularly fond of salami, Parma ham, olives and cheeses, and they're pretty knowledgeable about them, too.

It's a bit of a problem that we lost the butcher's shop and the greengrocer's, but I like being at this end of the town and we do very well here. There are a lot of interesting individual shops.

We'll get things in specially for people if we think they'll be popular and will fit in with our range. Our customers will often come in looking for one or two things, and they'll leave having bought five or six.

Rebecca and Simon at Beckworths.

The Rainbow café.

Plaques and signs in the High Street.

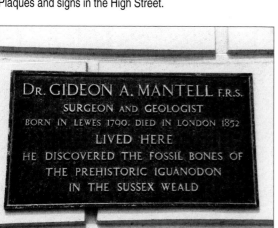

Bonne Bouche

Elizabeth Syrett, a Californian by birth, was Fortnum and Mason's chocolate buyer until, fifteen years ago, she bought a former Greek Orthodox bookshop in St Martin's Lane and created Bonne Bouche.

People say we're tucked away, but we're only a few yards from the High Street opposite the castle. There's an advantage in it, because my expenses would be much greater if I were in the High Street, and I'd have to pay staff. The whole thing would be a big operation, whereas I like to do it myself, with a lot of help from my husband John, who makes ice cream during the summer – there's strawberry, usually mango and pink grapefruit sorbet, and sometimes he might make banana, honey and yoghurt. There's raspberry, too, when they're cheap in the market, and pretty soon we'll be picking blackberries to make ice cream with that. It started in 1990, the last time we had really high temperatures as we're having this year, and people found it too hot for chocolate.

I go to about fifteen different suppliers to get chocolates which are really good of their kind. Most popular are the Belgian. The truffles are Charbonnel and Walker

(royal warrant, Tunbridge Wells!) and I get English creams from Audrey's in Hove – they're the most expensive chocolates that I buy. My busiest times are Easter and Christmas, and they're the only times you're likely to find queues, particularly for the Easter eggs. I buy the empty chocolate shells and fill them, to specification if required.

Champagne truffles are the most popular chocolate with Lewes people. They're the most alcoholic measure for measure. None of them are likely to intoxicate you, but you can get the flavour and it is very good. Children go for strawberry truffles, marzipan fruits, fruits de mer (sea shells) and anything colourful, although there are exceptions – one little boy always wants Bendincks bittermints.

Capriccio

Belinda Burton opened her ladies' clothes shop, Capriccio, twenty years ago.

Our clothes are practical, stylish, not hugely high fashion, but something a bit modern and a little different. The fabrics are mainly natural – a little bit of viscose, but no nylons and polyesters. These are clothes for women who can be who they want to be. The fashion isn't dictated to them off the magazine page.

There's a large artistic community here, and we're selling practical clothes with a slight artistic edge to them. It's not London: people don't want little short skirts and suits, and if they do they'll perhaps go to Next in Brighton. Most of our stuff is imported, unfortunately. A lot of good linen comes out of Europe, but most of our clothes are from the East. We don't have a Fairtrade policy, but the conditions of the people I buy from are very good – I used to visit them a lot. They're nicely built factories, they have lunch hours, they have loos and canteens and they have unions. They're not very well paid, but then in India nobody is. The point is that if there isn't a market in the West these people *will* starve.

The High Street has changed drastically since I first opened here. There are a lot more charity shops. The everyday goods shops such as the newsagents and the butchers have all disappeared because Tesco wasn't built far enough away. Safeway is at least in the town and part of it – you can just nip in – but people take their car to Tesco and do a major shop. I take my hat off to Bill, down in the Cliffe, who's managed to keep a really good vegetable shop and restaurant. We need more people like that.

Some seven or eight years ago the council gave up on the top end of the High Street. They said they were going to give planning permission for shops to be turned into homes, with the bottom end of town being commercial. It seems to me crazy to diminish the High Street when you have a massive parking problem. You'd have more circulation of traffic if you extended shopping the length of the street.

Shops have to be specialist to survive at this end of the High Street. We're the smart end, if you like. I don't get many browsers – people come in because they've made the effort. My customers are very loyal, and they bring their friends in, their daughters from London and their aunties from Reigate. There are several nice restaurants up here, and the shops will survive as long as the post office stays up here.

Adamczewski

Hélène Adamczewski has lived in Lewes for eighteen years, and four years ago she took over the former Lucy of Lewes shop in the High Street. Its contents, she admits, are not always obvious from the window display.

We just like to tease. It's a kind of set piece. It should be intriguing and interesting, and it should depict what we're about – a kind of simplicity. Whenever we get new things they more often than not go straight into the window, because that's our main showcase. People are uncertain about who we are and what we do. When we

first started people thought we were a gallery, and some find it intimidating to come in, although we're really friendly and helpful – I think we're lovely!

This is about having a different shopping experience. It's not like going into the pound shop or Boots or Debenhams where you know what you're going to get. We want people to come in and have an enjoyable experience exploring. We don't pounce on them. We let them discover. That seems to me to be the whole point of shopping – it should be a pleasurable experience.

We sell housewares, although there are exceptions to that, and our ethos is craftsmanship and functionality. I wouldn't say we cater for the expensive end of the market, because the emphasis is on quality – something that will last for ever, rather than for five minutes. We try to buy as much English stuff as we can, although that's becoming increasingly harder, and most of it is European. At the moment quite a bit comes from Belgium.

We have clients the length and breadth of the country, and now we're about to develop a mail order catalogue. We already send things to people. They ring up and say they've a wedding and would like suggestions for items that will fit their budget.

What's my favourite item in the shop at the moment? Well, I'm very fond of the Staffordshire jugs that we've got in the window, because there's a whole story behind that industry. Also they're made in the original Victorian moulds. This is the definitive jug: it does what it's supposed to do, and it's a fabulously crafted, mass-produced piece.

Edward Reeves

Tom Reeves is the fourth generation of a family which has spanned the history of photography in Lewes.

My great-grandfather moved to our present premises in 1858, by which time he was calling himself a watchmaker and jeweller and photographic artist. He was a photographer during the 1850s and photography as we know it was invented in 1852, so that means he was a pioneer. In theory we've kept all the negatives back to the beginning, but inevitably some of the glass plates have been broken or lost. Dad reckoned that there were about 200,000 images – 5 tons of glass plates – so we've got enough to be getting along with. The older, collodion ones have kept in mint condition. It's when you start getting into early gelatin, during the 1870s through to the 1920s and '30s, that they start to be a little less reliable.

I never seriously thought about doing anything else. Doctors breed doctors, don't they, and you grow up imbued with the atmosphere. Unfortunately when I was thirteen my father had some quite severe strokes, so I went off to college and learned it all there. I've been doing the job twenty years now, and I reckon I've just about got the hang of it.

The biggest change in those twenty years has been digital photography. My father stopped working in 1974, and at that stage we were telling people that we didn't recommend natural colour portraits, because it wasn't permanent – he was still agonising about the change from black and white to colour. By the time I started in 1982 everything was colour, certainly in the social field, and it wasn't a challenge because it was what I'd been trained in. It's only recently that film itself is becoming obsolete. You start to wonder whether you should invest in a new camera – should I wait until digital is that much more advanced and then completely re-equip? I'm already using digital for some commercial stuff: it's quicker

and just as good as film for most things. For a wedding, though, the thought of getting back home, putting the chip in the computer and learning that there's nothing on it is just too terrifying. I need to trust it more, but the time is coming.

My business is about 50 per cent social – weddings and portraits – and 50 per cent commercial, of which a fair bit is estate agency work. I think weddings are fairly constant and that there'll always be work for wedding photographers. The way the images are formed is going to change, with the coming of digital, but people will always want to end up with an album of photographs or photographs hung above the fireplace.

I don't take as many pictures as I should of the passing scene. My father took a lot of local views, and I've taken a few, but when I'm being chased six days a week for people who want their photographs taken it doesn't leave a lot of time for personal stuff. I'm very aware that there is this changing scene around us which should be recorded. I'm going to be found out when I retire, because someone will look at the negatives and ask 'Where are all the local views?' and there'll be a gap!

Pipe Passage is one of the many Lewes twittens.

The north side of the High Street showing Capriccio flanked by the Panda Garden Chinese restaurant and Jonathan Swann's jewellery business, The Workshop.

David Jarman

*Hidden away along Pipe Passage is David Jarman's second-hand bookshop.
It has no name, because he says he hasn't yet been able to think of one – and
therefore isn't in the telephone directory. In 1991 he started it as a private
library, with members paying an annual subscription which enabled them to
borrow new books as they came out.*

It seemed a good idea, because people complained that
the public library in Lewes was no longer meeting this
need. Twelve years later, however, I'm functioning as
a secondhand bookshop, although I do still have a few
elderly members. At its peak I had 120 members, but I feel
that a lot of them didn't use it anything like to the extent
they should have done, considering that they were paying
me a subscription. I have a feeling that many of them had
been badgered into joining by their friends.

My bookshop doesn't have a theme. Because I have
very small premises I buy the books one by one. I don't
buy them at auction, and I tend not to do house calls or
buy from members of the public – I have to warn them
that if they want to dispose of a lot of books, I'm only
going to be interested in buying a certain number of them,
and the rest wouldn't be easy to dispose of.

There are now seven or eight secondhand bookshops in Lewes, which is a lot more
than there were when I came to live in the town in 1984. Unlike the new book trade
it's a case of the more the better, because it becomes a place people visit for that
purpose. I get a lot of custom, especially at weekends, from Brighton, which was once
awash with secondhand book shops but now has far fewer than Lewes.

When it comes to costings, I must admit that like, I suspect, a lot of other businesses
in the High Street, it's not the kind of shop that someone who needs to make a lot
of money should open. The laws of economics, supply and demand, etcetera, don't
apply to many of them, or so I imagine. I sell quite a lot of books to other dealers,
and the stock is priced accordingly, so that it's equally attractive to specialist dealers
in something like modern first editions so that they can buy from me and sell on
through their catalogues.

One of the most depressing things about visiting other secondhand bookshops is
that you tend to see the same rather tired stock at the same inflated prices. Whereas
people used to mark up a book according to what they bought it for, there's now
a spurious notion that a book is worth a particular, universal price – presumably
somewhere there's a minor public schoolboy who dreamt up the figure in the first
place, but one doesn't quite know why. I buy stock that I'm fairly confident I can sell,
and I'm therefore happy to settle for a relatively small mark-up.

St Michael's church.

Sculpture on the church tower of St Michael's.

Brewers Arms sign.

WESTGATE
ONE WORLD CENTRE

Founded 1987
Oxfam/Traidcraft FairTrade Shop

*Meeting place for groups working
for justice, peace and responsible
stewardship of the Earth.*

OPENING TIMES:

Thursday . . 10·00a.m.- 12·30p.m.
Friday . . . . 10·00a.m.- 2·00p.m.
Saturday . . 10·00a.m.-12·30p.m.
Sunday . . . 11·30a.m. - 12·30p.m.

CLOSED IN AUGUST

For further information please telephone

477795 or 472172

Signs in the vicinity of the bottleneck. The satyr (left) is on the front of Bull House, an inn remodelled as a town house in 1583.

The 15th Century Bookshop at the bottleneck.

Full of Beans

Sara Gosling and her husband John have run their wholefood shop opposite the Westgate car park for twenty-five years.

We originally thought the shop might last for a few years, but it's just gone on and on. Unfortunately business has moved down to the other end of town, and up here you don't get the passing trade, which is sad – I couldn't have got by without our regulars. But if you can't beat them you have to join them – I take a stall at the

farmers' market in the Cliffe precinct once a month. We used to be next door, and in the really good times we had a double shop. Now we rent this shop and we've built ourselves a house next to our factory, by the Lewes Arms in Castle Ditch Lane. We make soya foods in the old Star Brewery bottling store – tofu, tempe, vegetarian quiches and all the things we sell here.

We try to get food which is as natural as possible and at the best price we can. Prices go up and down like yo-yos on fruits and nuts, because they're imported. Lewes people are quite adventurous, and they like the fact that they can bring a recipe in and will probably find what they're looking for, whether it's Japanese, Chinese, Indian, Malay or Indonesian. They can get the herbs and spices they need, and the right sort of rice, or noodles or oil.

Circa

Head chef Marc Bolger and his team have won rave reviews in the national quality press for their cuisine at Circa. Tamsin McLaren is manager of the restaurant, which was opened by Ashley and Ann Renton some four years ago.

The food is modern fusion, which means that we take eastern flavours and blend them with Mediterranean influences. Last year we won our first AA rosette, and we've had it confirmed again this year, but really we're happy if our customers are satisfied.

I think we sit quite nicely within the range of Lewes restaurants because we're so different from the others. You can eat Thai, Chinese, Indian and Italian, and we add that final touch. We're here for that special night out.

We also open at lunch time, and we know that people who may be in a hurry, or who don't want to spend too much money at lunch time, still want to have the Circa experience – a business lunch or a leisure lunch after shopping in the town.

Head chef Marc Bolger and manager Tamsin McLaren with their AA rosette.

We like being up here. We're close enough to the centre for people to walk to us, and we're quite lucky to have the Westgate car park next door. A lot of our customers come from the Brighton, Uckfield and Eastbourne areas, and we've been going from strength to strength every year.

12 St Anne's & Western Road

Tim & Liz Owen

Tim and Liz moved to St Anne's Hill from Lansdown Place in 1998. Tim is a computer manager, working in Croydon, while Liz has two part-time jobs, working for a charity and in the library service.

It's great for us living here, especially the house, which we fell in love with – it's a country cottage in the middle of the town. It has all the advantages of being in the country. You can wander out into the back garden and sit there, it's lovely; and we can walk out 50 yards and we're in the town with restaurants and shops. And the people who live here are great.

The houses vary in age. This one's getting on for 500 years, and the one next door is probably thirty years old – that's the sort of range. And bits of the house are different ages as well, because at one stage it was a very small house and then another bit was built on, and then we've built this extension since. It was once significantly outside the town walls, and there were many more houses in the area then. We've looked at the census of 1836, the first one recorded. Two of us live here now and don't regard it as a big house, but it was two houses and there were six people here. Quite a lot of the older houses in the town were built with stone from the Priory, but this one was built while the Priory was still there. Built of bits of rubbish really – wood, filled in with muck (wattle and daub) and covered with plaster.

We know nearly everybody. When it was the Jubilee celebrations last June we had a street party for St Anne's Hill and St Peter's Place. Anybody we didn't know before we got to know then. That helped the community feeling quite a lot.

There's an element of continuity. We've been here about five years. The person before us had lived here for twenty-six years so this is always their house. We asked at the street party when it becomes our house, and they said probably twenty years, but it's better if you die.

We were married just across the road in Shelleys. It was very nice to just stroll across and get married. It's a very nice place. We go there for meals, high days and holidays. Not cheap but great, and it's got better. The manager, Graham Coles, lives seven or eight houses up the road. We see him going past every day – the cleanliness of his shirts and how well pressed they are is always a great topic of conversation. We also have the Pelham Arms, which has changed hands a couple of times since we've been here, but which is now well established. It tends to be a young people's pub, with bands in the evenings, but it never causes any trouble.

We do a lot of our shopping at the butcher's and the greengrocer's in Western Road. They're both brilliant shops who'll do anything they can to help. We used to have a corner shop, but the nearest now are St Pancras and Leicester Road. But the two shops up there have started to sell bread and a lot of the basic things you'd go to a corner shop for, so you can actually manage to do most of your shopping in them. I'd say we do half our shopping there. They know all their customers by name. And they get what you want. You've only got to go into the greengrocer's and say 'Those are lovely, Vera' and the items tend to become more of a fixture, because she knows people like them. That's how shops are supposed to work.

It's a busy street commercially. There's a fish and chip shop, which we use now and then, and an undertaker's – which we haven't, but probably will in the end. The post office has closed, which is a shame. It's much nicer to go to a post office locally, and it helps other shops to survive. County Hall is just round the corner, and that probably keeps the sandwich shop going. And we've just had an antiquarian bookshop open up.

The Black Horse is just up the road (there's a bit of controversy because they've stopped stocking Harvey's beers). And Millers, opposite, is a very high class bed-and-breakfast place with four-poster beds – the sort of B&B that only Lewes could do, with beamed ceilings, chaise longues and four-poster beds. Absolutely fabulous.

This is a very good place to live on bonfire night, because you get the procession coming up and down – and you get everything twice. Talking of which, we shouldn't forget the Anglican and Roman Catholic churches facing each other across the street.

Shelleys

Graham Coles has been manager at Shelleys Hotel for fourteen years and has witnessed several changes of ownership in that period. This year it was bought by Peter and Sylvie Pattenden, who live in France – which means that Graham has total day-to-day responsibility:

The hotel is an extension of my private life to some extent. You couldn't do it on a 9 to 5 basis. You have to be available when the business demands it and when the customers expect to see you there. It can be anything up to eighty or ninety hours a week sometimes.

I like to think that we're providing a service that fits the community, and that locals will enjoy the hotel as much as visitors. While we're perhaps regarded as giving a de luxe standard of service – yes, we're the most expensive of the Lewes hotels –

Graham Coles in the garden at Shelleys.

we also give a personal service. I like to think of the hotel being used by local people as a meeting place. The bar, the restaurant, the lounge and the garden are all open to non-residents. Weddings are hugely important for us, and the garden at the back makes it a very attractive venue.

As for visitors, the Glyndebourne season is crucial. It's one of the prime reasons people come to Lewes, and the period from the middle of May until the end of August is a vital chunk of our year. We also get people who come here for conferences in Brighton and for Glyndebourne Touring Opera, and Christmas is a particularly busy period for us.

Lewes never has enough beds in the summer months. During the winter I think we could all improve our occupancy levels. It's frustrating when there's surplus space, and I feel that the town needs promoting more as a destination off-peak. For older people it's a good place to come for mid-week breaks. We have the antiques and the second-hand books, and we're very conveniently situated close to the Downs and the sea. There's Brighton, too. Many of our guests will stay here because they prefer to be in Lewes, but they'll nip down to Brighton, and it's important to have such a famous place on our doorstep.

The new owners and I have similar ideas about the way the business should be developed. Change was more difficult under company ownership, when spending was more tightly controlled. While we don't want to change the overall feel of the hotel, we certainly want to put some money back into refurbishment, maintaining the quality and perhaps being a little more individual. We'll be trying to use local suppliers for our food, for instance. There are plans for some extensions, although I don't know about the time-scale. We've planning permission for six more rooms – we have nineteen at present – and for a small conference room, too.

Lewes Old Grammar School, affectionately known as LOGS.

Pelham Arms sign.

The view up St Anne's Hill to the church.

St Pancras Roman Catholic church.

Iron grave markers in St Anne's churchyard.

Frank Richards

It was in 1932 that Frank Richards opened his butcher's shop in Western Road. His grandson Peter runs the business now – and some things haven't changed.

That cashier's kiosk in the corner has been there since the beginning, and we still use it. Once upon a time all butchers had them in order to separate the cash handler from the butcher for hygiene reasons, but we think that this one and another in Suffolk are the only ones left. It speeds business up. We tell the customers how much the meat is and they tell the cashier. Yes, of course we trust them.

Our meat is all locally produced. The beef comes from Ashcombe Farm on the A27 – you can almost see it from here, can't you? – the lambs are from Kingston and the chickens and pigs from Ditchling. We cure all our own bacon and cooked ham, and we make all our own sausages. We do more and more fancy ones. This week we've got Thai ones with lemon grass and fivespice. We've got an Old English one, whose recipe is supposed to be 200 years old. Most of them are gluten-free.

There were sixteen butchers' shops in Lewes before the war. We're the only original one left, and apart from that there's the one in the Riverside Centre and the supermarkets. I like to think we survive because we give the customers what they want. I certainly can't afford to retire yet.

Peter Richards with his partner Petrina Kingham.

Lewes Fruit Store

Vera Terry has run her greengrocer's business in Western Road for twenty-one years.

It's like a little village up here, a community of its own. Most of our trade is local, although we do get occasional passing trade. I sell as much local produce as I can. Someone bakes cakes for us, and we keep a range of Infinity Foods products. We sell all sorts of things. We're en route to the cemetery, so we sell loads of flowers for that, and at Christmas time we have trees and holly wreaths.

I was very sorry to see the post office go. Every time we lose a shop it's a blow. It's a case of hanging on in and hoping we're able to keep going here. The butcher and I complement each other. He's selling stamps now, and I'm selling matches, because we don't have a newsagent any more. If people ask for something I'll try to get it at the cash-and-carry.

There are only three greengrocers left in the whole of Lewes now – me, Bill's in the Cliffe and Swanborough Nurseries in Fisher Street. It's a lot of hard work and worry to keep going. I start at 7 and finish at about a quarter past 5, and of course there's all the book work when you're self employed. I'd like to retire soon, although my customers say they won't let me.

The post office has closed, but Western Road retains a core of highly valued shops.

The Black Horse, Western Road, which has controversially decided not to stock Harvey's beers.

The Pewter Pot pub in Western Road changed its name to the Meridian, the 0° longitudinal line passing close by. There is another marker on the Landport estate (see page 24).

The Greenwich Meridian Passes Through This Point

Plaque placed
by Town Mayor
Clr. M.S Breese
July 1975
to Commemorate
the Tercentenary
of the
Royal Observatory
and
European Heritage
Year

Western Road, north side: a new development on the site of the former Caffyns garage.

13 Malling

Maureen & David Messer

The Messers have lived in Lewes for twenty-two years. Maureen has twice been mayor of Lewes during a sixteen-year spell on the town council, and she has also been chairman of the district council, on which she served as a Liberal Democrat for eight years. David is a retired policeman, and was for several years beat policeman on the Landport, Nevill, Wallands and Ousedale estates.

D: Malling is two estates really. There's the older area around here, which includes Hereward Way, Spence's Lane and the Lynchetts, and the new estate on the other side of Malling House, which is now the police headquarters. These houses were built about the 1950s. Before then it was a typical country estate, with Malling House as the manor, with fields and orchards all around. Then it all got sold up. The police took over the building and new houses were put up as married quarters for the police and the prison service. Today they've been sold off, and so you've got a mixed bag between private and council-owned houses. The big worry, with house prices so high in the town, is that young people can't afford to stay here when they grow up and have families.

   M: The estate originally had just one access road, but once it began to grow they had to think about the consequences of some two thousand more people moving in, most of them with cars. The road into town was regularly jammed – you could spend three quarters of an hour getting out. The initial plans were to knock down homes and put a new access road right through the middle of the estate, but they eventually created Mayhew Way, and that, to us, seems the right decision – even if the bridge does pass just above our house.

   D: The estate itself has a limited number of facilities. We've got a small grocery shop, a sub-post office and a hairdresser's, Simply Hair. The shop carries only a limited supply of things, so most people go into the centre and use Tesco or Safeway. We've got the advantage of having footpaths across the Malling playing fields, and there's a local bye-law which allows people to cycle along them, too. Any special functions, such as birthday parties, weddings and so on, are held at the community centre. That started off about twenty-seven years ago as a hall and a small bar, but over the years they've extended it. There's a youth club and changing rooms for football, and there are plans for a skateboard park nearby as well. You see youngsters with them all over town – at the back of Safeway, by the law courts, along the streets among the traffic – and hopefully they'll sort something out soon. But nothing can happen until the authorities have decided what flood defences are going to be put across the area, and that could take a very long time.

M: The floods of 2000 were devastating, and I never want to see another thing like that in my lifetime. The water was up to 9ft in the houses in Spence's. People were brought to the community centre by the police and the coastguards. We were there for a week and we looked after hundreds of people each day. I'm chairman of the flood action group, and three years on we've got nothing. It's appalling. The Environment Agency to my knowledge has spend nearly £2 million talking about it. They say the river's been brought back to the standard before the flood happened. The authorities are endlessly argey-bargeying and we're getting nowhere. We're going up to London with our scientific officer to see Defra about it. I'm talking to you during the last week of July 2003 and the last person is being rehoused this week – nearly three years later.

The Messers in their garden, with the raised roadway of Mayhew Way behind them.

St Michael the Archangel

Brian King, an Australian, is acting vicar of South Malling church, St Michael the Archangel, for a year. He arrived here with his wife Pamela in February 2003.

I was bishop for western Sydney, and it's compulsory there to retire at sixty-five, which for me was the end of January. I have a family here in London – son and daughter-in-law and granddaughter – and when the local bishop knew I was going to be free he said I should contact him before I committed myself anywhere else, and that's how we've found ourselves here.

Sydney Church of England is basically low church evangelical, and the chemistry here is very happily matched to that. In English terms it's pretty low church, but it's still dignified and liturgical and recognisably Church of England. I've been

door-knocking around the estate, one house after another, telling people that the local church is alive and well, and that leads me to many interesting conversations on doorsteps. I'd like to think that people are aware that there is a church in South Malling. Numbers have been increasing since I came here. We had about twenty-five at first and it's thirty-five or forty now. There's a bit of confidence building up.

I understand that about fifteen or twenty years ago it was a very vigorous church, with youth work here for teenagers and play groups for young mothers with toddlers. Because of a change of personnel that's largely fallen away, and the involvement with young families has been taken up by the local school and the South Malling community centre, where there are a lot of playgroups. However, the church is pivotal to the Malling estate, because it's identified as *the* church here, and I understand that the local bishop has plans to revive our involvement with youth work from next year. When I go to the school I'm so impressed with the number of prams that mothers bring as they drop their children off at school. There are a lot of young families in the Malling estate, and the door is wide open for inviting them to enter into the benefits of Christianity for the sake of their children and their family life.

We'll be taking back very happy memories. The church folk have been so welcoming to a roving, retired Sydney bishop. They've loaned us furniture for the vicarage, for example. I'm on no salary here: it's house-for-duty only.

Lewes is a lovely town, and very historical. In my studies of church history, when I was leaving accountancy to become a clergyman, I read up all about the 1500s and early 1600s in early English church history, and how the Puritans broke away, wanting freedom from the established church. Then I came here to South Malling to find that this building had been in ruins for a hundred years after the Dissolution, but that a Puritan businessman bought it and rebuilt it, and in 1626 here it was open again as a Puritan stronghold – and it was quite moving for me to be standing here in the pulpit of the Puritan heritage that I'd read about.

Of course, I've heard all about the great bonfire night on 5 November. I haven't seen it yet – but I'll be there!

Malling Community Centre.

14 South Street

David Sykes

A retired teacher, David Sykes lives with his wife Anne in the house built for the master of the former workhouse next door. A mountaineer when young, he remains a keen sailor, and his catamaran is moored close to Cliffe Bridge. The couple have lived in Lewes for thirty years and in South Street for fourteen years.

The first thing that struck me about this end of town when I came here was that it had its own microclimate. It's to do with this steep west-facing cliff behind us – either the cold north-easterly winds fly right over the top, or the westerly winds form an air barrier against the cliff. I regularly come up the Ouse in my boat in a strong westerly, and as soon as I get near to the quarries and under the railway bridge the wind drops. There can be a gale blowing out to the west, and it is exposed, but this barrier forms and the air leaves the ground and goes over the top before it gets to the cliff. Whenever you walk down the street, coming from anywhere in Lewes, you just feel that increase in temperature. It's probably only one or two degrees, but it's noticeable.

David Sykes on board his catamaran.

The other thing we first noticed was the continual presence of seagulls, which love the cliff and do a lot of soaring overhead. They give an air of holiday to the place. Of course we're very close to the Downs here – five minutes up Chapel Hill and you're up on the top – and just round the corner is the Railway Land nature reserve.

The river is very much a part of the street when you get to the far end, by the Snowdrop. People look at photographs taken from the opposite river bank, looking back towards South Street and the sailing club, and they ask 'Where is this lovely place?' And we say it's the scruffy old River Ouse and it's the south end of Lewes. I used to be a member of the sailing club, but my boat's too big for that. The lovely thing about the club is that it's a proper local artisans' sailing club – it's not at all 'yachty', expecting people to wear silly clothes and pose around.

They've got their own workshops there, and many of them are amateur engineers and so on.

The Snowdrop was done up so splendidly by Tim and Sue that I absolutely loved it. They had a profound effect on the whole ethos of the pub. There were all sorts of wonderful, mad, gorgeous things to be seen there. A lot of the most interesting out-of-work young people in Lewes found the Snowdrop a natural home – a lot of them were the sort who'd opted out of the rat-race. The pub has just had a change of ownership, so it's too soon to say what differences there'll be.

That's at one end, while at the other you've got our excellent fish-and-chip shop. It gives a lovely balance. The shame is that we haven't got a corner shop, because otherwise this would be like a small village. We did have one or two restaurants, which we've lost, but there are plenty within easy reach. One of the most popular shopping districts in the whole area is just round the corner in Cliffe, and it's all on the level. You don't need to use a car. Mind you, we do get young men in cars driving up and down here much too fast despite the fact that it became a cul-de-sac when the Cuilfail Tunnel was built.

As for the community, we've got plenty of Lewes people who still live down here. One of the nice things for many of us is that in the last five or six years many more young children have come to the street, and some early teenagers, too. Sure, sometimes the skateboards can be a bit noisy, but it's lovely. We've a great active bonfire society, and we also have a well above average sprinkling of musicians, authors, artists and people in the media. It really is a very interesting mix, and we all get on very well.

People helped each other a lot during the floods. We had boats moored to lampposts, and it was just like being in Venice. We had some of the old people in our house, because we were above the flood water, but the police said everybody had to go. We took them down our side passage and they stepped straight into a boat which went off down the river in the street. I got rolled over three times canoeing down Cliffe High Street to check on my boat, and I'm an old surf kayak instructor – quite shaming, that was!

I'm also pleased that we've got Chandlers the builders' merchants just round the corner. People grumble about the lorries, but the place is full of local artisans and tradespeople, many of them my old pupils with whom I enjoy passing the time of day. I can just go round with a wheelbarrow and load up with bricks and cement or whatever else I need. South Street's a totally different environment from living on a housing estate. Sometimes I think it's got a French feel. When you stand at the end of the street and look down it, with its wonderful mixture of old houses, it just feels continental.

The Snowdrop

D'Arcy Gander and his wife Tanya bought the Snowdrop a few months ago.
He says it was a temptation too great to resist.

I grew up in Lewes and lived here until I was about seventeen years old. I lived predominantly in the Cliffe area, around Harvey's Brewery, lived in South Street off and on and got to know the Snowdrop well. I've been in the pub trade for about five years – I've got the Belle Vue in Brighton and the Freemasons Tavern in Hove – and when I heard that this was coming on the market I thought 'Let's go for it'.

The Snowdrop's always been very bohemian, and that appeals to me. It's had a funky feel, and I like to do things a little bit differently myself. The ambience of the place is brought about by the decor. It has a lot of bric-a-brac in it – quirky and unusual things. I'm streamlining it a little bit, but I've still got Indonesian carvings and various objects which give it a nautical feel, being close to the river. Most of them

are left over from Tim and Sue May, the previous incumbents, but we're in the process of doing a lot of work ourselves. We've just finished renovating the function room upstairs, and that's going to have a Chinese theme. I'm importing some furniture from Shanghai for that.

We're keeping a strong emphasis on food – we have five chefs here, and the food's got a strong vegetarian focus. We try to use local suppliers. The meats that we do use come from a supplier over by Heathfield, and it's all hormone-free, additive-free and free range wherever possible. We were featured in the *Daily Telegraph* a few weeks ago – a very good review.

The pub appeals to a very broad cross-section. Jazz has been running here on Monday nights for eight or nine years, and we'll keep the live music going. We have three or four events every month. Apart from music aficionados we get ramblers, a lot of young people, especially on Friday nights, and a growing number of thirty- and forty-somethings with their children.

We're changing the pub sign – that's why it's missing at the moment. The old one was a traditional hand-painted hand sign, showing the avalanche which gives the pub its name. A friend of mine painted it, but it had been up there about fifteen years and it was somewhat weather-beaten. The new one will still refer to the avalanche, but it will have more of a cartoon style.

Lewes Rowing Club

Peter Thorpe, born in Lewes sixty-seven years ago, has been intimate with the River Ouse all his life and is a long-time member of the rowing and sailing club.

We've got about 160 members and there are sixty-three boats, so some are non-boat-owning members. It's a working men's club as we see it. It was built by the people who worked for the railway, the river board and the cement works. Several of the shop owners in Lewes used to own boats here.

We don't find it hard to get new members, but you have to pick out those who are going to be an advantage to you – those who don't just want to find somewhere convenient to dump a boat. After all, when they become a member they own a part of the club, so you pay the penalty if you allow people in who don't want to contribute to it properly.

There isn't any commercial fishing done here. We've tried to stop the club being taken over in that way. We've also resisted people who want to buy the land to develop it. It would be worth a lot of money, but we decided there was nowhere on the river we could go and get what we've got here. We could attach moorings somewhere else, but we wouldn't own the access or enjoy the same security.

We're not an expensive club. My fee for a boat over 20ft is £146 a year, and trailerised members with boats under 20ft pay £110, so that's not bad, is it?

Offshore fishing was always good from Seaford through to Beachy Head. The area's well known for the Channel whiting. Just recently they've tailed off a bit because of over-fishing. Cod and bass have suffered, too. But we just go out for a day's sport really.

There used to be some good eels in the river. There still are, but if they're overfished for two or three seasons it takes some time for numbers to grow again. But the mullet in this river seem to be on the increase – there are thousands of them.

Peter Thorpe painting Star One.

South Street Fish Bar

Kostas Economou and his wife took over the running of the fish and chip shop from her parents in 1990.

Our main trade are the locals, because there's no passing trade along this road. There's not even any parking here, but people will stop outside for a while and that's not a problem. But we do get regulars coming from the towns and villages around, too.

Cod and chips is the main seller here – that's the great British tradition. There aren't so many fish about, so we're charged more for them, but we can't put our own prices up because we've got a regular clientele. We don't make any money on the fish. We just about break even on fish and make our profit on chips, sausages and pies.

We've introduced curry sauce in the last two or three years. We've a lot more northerners living in the south these days, and they asked us to put it on the menu. The same goes for mushy peas.

Bags of Books

The popular children's bookshop was founded by Angela McPherson in 1991. Paul and Rachel Waller took over the business a few months ago. Rachel was a primary teacher and Paul was in banking.

The margins are very small, and you have to work very hard at it, but books gives people a lot of pleasure and we think it's a business that can be expanded. The building helps to give an atmosphere of old-world service and charm. There are probably only about thirty shops in the whole country that specialise in children's books, and people like the range we're able to carry. We have many titles, but few in number – we'll often buy in ones and twos.

It's hard to compete with the chains, but we did sell the latest Harry Potter. You try to differentiate the service a little bit. We were prepared to deliver it, and we put an owl feather in it and wrapped it up and tried to get it there early in the morning.

The Horowitz books are very popular. Children buy Roald Dahls every single day. Lemony Snickett is a recent one that's done very well. Lots of fantasy, of course, in the wake of Harry Potter. The traditional books are still selling, too – Enid Blyton, and classics like *Sleeping Beauty* and *Treasure Island*, and other books we grew up with.

Some children buy one or two books a week and come back week after week after week. We get a lot of enquiries from parents: 'My child is a relunctant reader; how can I encourage him?' They go off with an armful of books, and you hope you've chosen wisely for them and that we've been the trigger for that child becoming a reader.

It's encouraging to see how many children do read books. We've seen tiny ones on the floor with a book off the shelf and reading out loud. Fantastic! We'd like a shop double the size, with room to have the books displayed face-out, because the artwork is so good.

We'd like to expand into more schools in Sussex for the teachers coming to us. Term times are very, very busy for teachers – and you find *them* sitting on the floor going through the boxes of books and waxing lyrical about new titles!

Nutty Wizard

Paul Davey is summer coordinator of the Lewes community café, Nutty Wizard – in the former public lavatories on the corner of South Street and Cliffe High Street. A registered charity, it is supported by donations from local companies and individuals.

It's run as a café for the whole community, but our main priority is youth. The idea is to give the children of the town a place to meet rather than hang about the streets. It gives them a chance to be more hands-on, because we get them to work in the kitchen and serve people behind the counter, so that everyone who uses the café is involved in the running of it. They think to themselves, 'This is our café, our project'. We've got computer games, music and snooker, and sometimes we've tried to do more educational things at the All Saints Centre, too – but we ran out of volunteers this summer.

In our initial literature we said we were catering for young people between the ages of twelve and twenty-five, but we've got eight-year-olds in here today and we don't usually get anyone much above sixteen. Once one group finds us their friends

will often start coming, and that will last until they grow up. I started coming in 2000 with my friends, and we've all gone to university now – I'm at Oxford Brookes. But we also get lots of adults, because of the food that we do. We offer a full English breakfast for £2, and we usually put chairs and tables outside.

We don't offer a child-minding service, but parents are happy to leave their children here for a while, knowing that they'll be safe, dry and fed. There are play parks and the Pells, but you'd have to have an adult responsible for you there. Over the summer we're open from 11 until 5. During term time we open on Wednesday and Friday evenings and all day Saturday and Sunday.

We're very strict about drugs and alcohol. Conversations about drugs are stopped straight away. We're not too keen on violence, threatening behaviour and verbal abuse, but we have a fairly laid-back attitude: 'Why are you doing this?' We have a chat about it. We have trustees who oversee the running of the place. They're very diplomatic, and they'll speak to the children and the parents if they have to. It's very rare that we ban somebody. After all, they're children, and they will make mistakes – it would be stupid to have a 'lock 'em up and throw away the key' mentality. You get the odd idiot, but they're a really good bunch of kids.

15 Southover

Peter Gough

Peter Gough and his late wife came to Southover forty years ago when he was a physics master at Brighton College. He is now retired, and has taken up sculpting in flint.

Southover has changed very little over the years. The people are inclined to be very friendly. Perhaps a half of them are commuters of some sort, if only to Brighton. The traffic has increased, of course, and heaven knows where we'd be without the bypass. The traffic calming is dreadful, but I don't see how it could possibly be helped. Before the bypass it was possible to take a short walk and be immediately in the country.

This is a village. We've pubs at either end, the King's Head and the Swan, and our church, St John's. It's a popular church: people come in from Rodmell, Ringmer and so on. It's a very low church actually – a bit too low for my taste – but it has a Prayer Book communion every Sunday morning, and that suits me to a T. The old vicar was a wonderful man, and a real friend, but I'm pleased to say that the new vicar's a delightful chap, too.

Across from me is Anne of Cleves House. It's a busy place, and they have weddings there. We've also got Grange Gardens – lovely, apart from the awful municipal flowers. We're very lucky to have it.

The local shop in St Pancras is wonderful, invaluable. I haven't got a car, and in any case I wouldn't go near a superstore because I hate the idea of them. They'll get you anything you want. I've even tried the curries occasionally, although I'm not particularly fond of Indian food. They're delightful people and a terrific help.

Until recently we had a post office which was the centre of village life. It wasn't just a matter of buying stamps. William knew if people were ill, and he'd help them in all sorts of ways. That was just wonderful – exactly how a village should work. Now you have to go to the main post office, with huge queues and no sort of sympathy. If you forget your money you've had it, but when I did that with William occasionally there was no problem at all. That's the difference between being known and not being known.

People are very friendly here. Whether you're a professor at the university or Tom, Dick or Harry you're accepted, just as in a village. People are concerned about their neighbours even if they don't know them very well. That's Southover.

I retired at sixty and decided that I wanted to be a sculptor, but I couldn't think of a medium that was cheap enough. Then I hit on the idea of using flints, which I could pick up in the fields for nothing. I stick them together. I haven't made much money from them, but I do sell them, and the people who buy them are satisfied customers – they find they come to like them more rather than less. They see more in them.

Peter with one of his flint sculptures.

The Old Post Office

William Garrett's post office in Priory Street was closed down in June 2003.
At the age of seventy-two, and after twenty-five years, he was ready to retire –
but he says he'd kept it going because of the service it provided.

The post office was a focal point here. People were shocked when it closed. I hadn't realised they thought so much of my wife and me being here – the response was amazing. It's part and parcel of running a small post office that you help people outside of the business itself, and they seem to have appreciated that. Now they've got to go all the way up to the High Street.

As for me, I've suddenly got a lot of time on my hands. I haven't got used to that yet.

Pelham Terrace – the finest terrace in Lewes.

Anne of Cleves House.

King's Head pub sign.

Swan pub sign.

St John's church.

Grange Gardens Café

Drina Witham, a qualified caterer, has run the café in Grange Gardens for the past two seasons, helped by her daughter Hannah and a team of students.

We're open every day from the beginning of March until the end of October if the weather is good enough. It's a lovely place to be – I just love the tranquillity of it.

I sell teas, soft drinks, ices, home-made cakes and sandwiches, and it's always very busy when the sun shines. Carrot cake's the favourite.

St Pancras Stores

Chaula Patel and her husband Janak have owned their shop for the last ten years, and are best known for the curries she cooks.

I began with the traditional vegetarian recipes of Gujarat, but later I adapted recipes from other regions of India. At first only a handful of people bought them, but word of mouth had its effect and before long I was preparing 300 dishes every three weeks and there were long queues outside the shop on Friday evenings. Now I freeze them, and thanks to Alan Wyle at Action in Rural Sussex (which used to be the Sussex Rural Community Council) I sell into twenty-five village shops throughout the county. I'm hoping for planning permission so that I can buy the Stoyan restaurant in Station Street and run a take-away service there.

We've extended the shop, and we like to stock items that people can't find elsewhere – unusual things. We sell local eggs and wines, as well as Infinity Foods products.

Yes, we're related to the Patels on Landport and in Leicester Road. We're taking over Lewes!

16 St Nicholas Lane

John Geering

Four generations of the Geering family have lived in St Nicholas Lane. John lives at no. 42 with his wife, Shirley.

We've always been signwriters and painters, and we were grainers, too. Most of the graining was for the pub trade, but we also worked on shop fronts and house doors. We'd make up a scumble stain of white spirit, lindseed oil and terebin which we'd scrub onto the wooden surface before using metal combs and badger floggers to imitate a variety of grains. Some of our work can still be seen in the town hall and corn exchange, as can our heraldry on the ceilings and walls. Over the years we've updated a lot of their honours boards.

St Nicholas Lane used to be a mixture of commercial and residential. When you came in at the top, Stone's the bakery stood on the right-hand corner, with a tea room. The workmen would sneak in there and have their lunch in the back part of the shop. On the opposite corner was Flint's the grocers, now Flint House. You could always smell the roasting coffee, which was wonderful. As you progressed down the lane you came to Wightman and Parish's warehouse on your right, with the rear window shaped as if it belonged to a church. They kept their paints, polishes, aerosol canisters and paraffin in there, as well as china and pottery from, I believe, the Dicker Potteries, but unfortunately there was a disastrous fire and it burned down. Next there was the back entrace to T.G. Roberts, the grocers in the High Street, followed by a row of white cottages where my family still lives. Next to these was the stable for Flint's the grocer's and then another large warehouse belonging to Wightman and Parish, which housed the baths, toilet fittings and other heavy goods. On delivery day the street would fill up with loose straw – no bubble wrap in those days.

Opposite was a pub, the Dolphin Inn, a Page and Overton's house – a lovely old pub, much used in earlier days when the market was in the High Street. The jockey boys stayed overnight in the attic during Lewes Races days. It had a very low ceiling, but that suited them as they weren't very tall. My uncle and cousin took this building over for their signwriting business, and when my cousin retired we in turn extended our firm into this building. In the scullery was a very deep brick-lined well. We lowered a lamp down to 70ft before we hit rubble – it had been filled in. The water table is down in Friar's Walk, so the well would have been very deep indeed. Some winters we'd find water in the bottom.

Further down the lane was Baxter's, the printworks, which closed more than a year ago. They had a big old warehouse which extended to the edge of the road and over the electricity substation. Past the warehouse were three old flint cottages, and they were derelict. Baxter's used them for storage. They had a lead-lined wooden trough in the garden of one of them. They kept acid in there, and they used it to clean the ink rollers from the presses. There was a Plymouth Brethren chapel next door. They used to meet three times a day, and the pastor was the foreman-mechanic of Rugg's garage, which was opposite. It was a very large garage, but it had a very low roof, so they couldn't take in commercial vehicles. They used to run coaches, which they called Rugg's charabancs in those days. Baxter's suffered a disastrous fire in the 1950s. The chapel was pulled down after that, and the factory was rebuilt and extended. Rugg's later closed down and the Caburn Court flats were built on the site.

After the chapel you came to another of my family's workshops, where we used to do all the coach-painting. We'd paint, spray and write the signs for trucks and vans – even prams – and we did car repairs, too. Autopaints is in there today. There'd once

John and Shirley Geering. Her passion is the garden. His are the Greek costumes he researches, makes and wears for the Waterloo procession on bonfire night. 'The transverse horse-hair crest on the Corinthian helmet, which was worn by the Spartans, is a sign of rank for officers. That's fifth century. The other is a Phrygian helmet worn by the Macedonian army during the time of Alexander the Great.'

been a knacker's yard on the site, and they used to bring up the cattle for slaughter there when they held the Monday markets over at Southover. They said blood used to run down the street to the bottom.

Below it is Rose Cottage, quite a large house with a garden, and then – on both sides of the lane – you've a series of small cottages. There was a grocer's shop on the corner with Lansdown Place.

When the lane was largely commercial it was a chaotic lane as regards the delivery of goods. The street used to be blocked for hours on end, even until recent years. Deliveries would start at about 5.30, and there'd be anything up to six trucks in the lane at one time. The industry has all but gone now, apart from ANB Signs – who are in my old workshop, the business being sold to Andrew Brownings – and the paintshop near the bottom. There's also a mews in the car park which was formerly Wightman and Parish's, and there's a firm of accountants upstairs. Underneath is my studio, where I make bonfire costumes. My hobby is making ancient Greek, Scythian and Roman armour, and I design and write the banners for my society, which is the Waterloo Bonfire Society.

We all know each other at the top of the lane, and we'll sometimes meet in each other's houses. I don't know everyone at the bottom, but Russell Beck is a friend of mine: he runs a prop design company, supplying theatres in London. Baxter's and Caburn Court divide the street, and the two mini communities are generally referred to as top- and bottom-enders.

The view down St Nicholas Lane with the Downs as a backdrop.

Top Enders

Caroline and Christopher Dorling

The Dorlings live in Flint House with their nineteen-year-old son Henry and their Cavalier King Charles Spaniel Leo. Christopher was a founder of the Dorling Kindersley publishing house, while until three years ago Caroline ran a widely known natural health centre in the building.

Caroline: We had about sixteen therapists working here and used to run workshops and courses as well, which was quite unusual – especially as we attracted people with an international reputation to run them. The place was humming all day, all evening and at weekends. It was very exciting, and people felt it was part of the community. Although it was avant garde when we started it, by the time I closed it twelve years later attitudes to complementary medicine and the things that I'd pioneered here were commonplace.

When we reached the year 2000 people asked what I was going to do for the millennium, and I realised that I'd given the project as much as I had left to give – I was pretty much worn out. I tried to sell it as a going concern, but after a deal had fallen through for the fourth time Christopher came up with the idea of selling our family home and turning Flint House into a town dwelling.

When I started running the natural health centre full time I had to give up things like my wood turning, and now I've started it up again. I work in the cellar. I've joined a wood-turning group – they were full, but they made an exception for me because I'm a woman, and it means that I get a lot of tips, some nice bits of wood and invitations to a lot of workshops!

I've shown in three exhibitions in the last few weeks, including one at the Star Gallery and Gill Autie's Open House during Artwave. This piece is made of beech. It was an insignificant piece of wood, but I could tell that there was something quite interesting happening with the grain, which came to life after shaping and polishing.

Christopher: I started Dorling Kindersley with Peter Kindersley – and Caroline – in 1974. For about six or seven years it operated as a packaging company, which meant that we didn't actually publish things ourselves but sold to other publishers all over the world. The idea right from the beginning had been to create illustrated books that could be sold internationally, and I think we probably did that in a way that had never been achieved before. By the time I left there were probably 120 employees, which in publishing terms is quite a large number.

I sold my 50 per cent stake in the company in 1987, because my long-held ambition had been to move out of London by the time I was fifty to pursue other interests I had when a boy. Working on the land was one of these. We bought a country house with 10 acres in East Sussex. Most of it we turned into a garden, but after the hurricane of 1987, when we lost a lot of large trees, my reaction was to take woodland management courses at Plumpton College and plant a 3-acre deciduous wood. Thirteen years later it had developed to such an extent that it needed a great deal of work in the way of thinning and coppicing – the trees were 20 to 30ft high. When we sold the house and garden in order to move to Flint House we kept the wood and since then I've been spending most of my time working there.

Since moving into Lewes I've also put a great deal of time and effort into a local youth music project called Starfish. Young people aged between nine and nineteen come once a week and play in rock bands. In any year about a hundred young people come to one of our courses, composing their own music, recording themselves and, most important of all, performing regularly in front of large public audiences in Lewes and elsewhere locally.

The project has grown to such an extent that we operate on three evenings a week during term time. It began in rooms at the YMCA building, but at the beginning of this year we moved to Priory School where, very generously, the school have given us their music department to ourselves for the three evenings. This enables us to have up to five bands all performing at the same time. I'm not sure what it does for my ears, but it's wonderful to see how young people grow in confidence and self-esteem and in pure technical excellence. Very recently we put on a concert at All Saints Arts Centre by musicians who had been at Starfish back in 1998 when we started the project, and we managed to have 25 per cent of the first intake performing again, playing as semi-professionals now. That was an extremely rewarding evening.

D'Arcy Bleiker and Anna Burford

D'Arcy and Anna, the most recent incomers to the top end of the street, are both opera singers.

Anna: I'm a mezzo soprano. I've worked for Welsh National Opera and English National Opera, and I've sung *Orfeo* in Strasbourg. I was booked to sing Hansel in *Hansel and Gretel* for Welsh National Opera, but I've had to cancel because I'm expecting a baby in January.

This country's struggling a bit in the opera field, and Europe's starting to feel the pinch. There used to be so many houses in Germany, but they're starting to close down. America's the place to be, because that's where the money is – corporate sponsors. We've both got work coming up in Seattle (D'Arcy in 2005 and me a year later), so hopefully we'll get a few more jobs out there and stay a bit longer.

D'Arcy: I'm a bass baritone, and I've sung at Glyndebourne and the Royal Opera House. The low point in my career was bursting a blood vessel in a vocal chord twenty minutes before I was due to appear in the Cardiff Singer of the Year competition this year: I was absolutely gutted.

Yes, I think the neighbours have got used to hearing us rehearsing. We try not to start too early in the morning!

Kevin McSweeney

Kevin McSweeney is an antiques dealer, with a stall in the antiques centre in Cliffe High Street. He supplements his income by selling at auctions, and he also does a small part-time job for Gorringe's the auctioneers.

Business is difficult. You'd think there'd be a plethora of things. Yes, there *is* plenty of stuff, but a lot of it isn't what you'd call antique. Lewes isn't one of my main sources, although I sell here.

This is a Georgian honey jar. At some stage it suffered a slight crack, and some enterprising person has mended it by putting a silver rim around it and tightening up the cracks. It makes it in a way more interesting.

The Arscott family

Jill and David Arscott live with their children Rosie (right), Jack and Beth at no. 51. Jill is a freelance journalist. David is a writer, broadcaster and publisher – and the author of this book.

Andy and Penny Brownings

Andy and Penny Brownings live at no. 46. He runs the ANB sign-writing business in St Nicholas Lane, while Penny has worked for the Cliffe Veterinary Group since 1994.

Penny: I specialise in horses, doing anaesthesia and radiography. Although the practice is based in Cliffe High Street, I'm head nurse at the equine clinic in Laughton – we have fully functional operating, diagnostic and instensive care facilities there.

I'm an avid rider myself. The worst thing that's happened to me was being kicked nastily in the hip and ending up in hospital. Yes, I forgave him.

Andy: I worked for John Geering for twenty years, and when he retired four years ago I took over the business from him. Most of our work is in the town. We get a lot by word of mouth, and we do jobs for the local authorities, police, fire brigade etcetera.

It's changed quite a lot over the last four or five years. About 90 per cent of it's computerised now and the rest hand-painting, whereas before it was the other way round. But we keep the sign-writer on, because, the town being as old as it is, there's still a call for traditional work to be done on shop fronts. I do some of them myself.

Which job have I been particularly pleased with? Harvey's Brewery – all round the top of it is 24 carat gold leaf on black aluminium. It can be seen from anywhere in the town. We did it fifteen years ago, and we've recently redone it, plus all the gold work down at Harvey's depot. I'm very proud of those.

A Man in the Middle

Derek Lamport

Derek Lamport, who lives in Caburn Court, is a Sussex man who retired to Lewes after being research professor at Michigan State University. He is now a visiting senior research fellow at the University of Sussex.

I'm a plant biochemist with a special interest in the plant cell wall, trying to explain how plants grow, at a basic molecular level. In fact I think we're on the verge of a very nice breakthrough. It's arcane sort of stuff, but our last couple of papers, which I'm just finishing off, are milestone papers, seminal.

Will the research be of any use? There are always practical results. It's like Hertz who discovered radio waves. He said 'This is an example of something which has no use whatsoever' – and we all know rather better now. And who imagined when Watson and Crick discovered the structure of DNA that it would have so many applications? They opened Pandora's box.

The redundant Baxter's factory.

Bottom Enders

Sue Hamilton

Sue Hamilton, an archaeologist, came to live at no. 10 some three years ago.

I work at the Institute of Archaeology in London, which is part of University College, and I look at the later prehistory of Britain and Europe, from 2000 BC to the Romans. I do quite a lot of field work in Sussex.

This is the first time I've ever lived in a town. There's another archaeologist next door, Mike Seager Thomas, and that's why I came here – I knew it was an interesting place before I moved. It's one of those invisible streets. Once you come into the houses and look into the gardens you discover that they have characters of their own which nobody would suspect from the outside. Two down from here there was a stained glass artist who worked in the privy, and I have an almost perfect privy myself – the last original one in the lane.

I like the fact that it's a working lane. It is pretty, but there's lots of industry going on. I quite like the silence now that Baxter's has closed, but I'd much rather have an industrial building there than more houses. There's always been a bit of industry mixed in.

The people are interesting. I had some French visitors who said it was just like a village, with everyone knowing everyone else. I don't think there's a 'normal' person in the street. I don't know everyone's job, but I don't regard being an archaeologist as normal. We've got opera singers, we've got John Geering who's always up to all sorts of things, we've got Dave opposite who's really keen on his bikes, and at the end of this little group of cottages we've got Rebecca with her bizarre window, always decorated oddly. It's full of character.

Dave and Polly Robinson

The Robinsons live at Rose Cottage, down at the bottom end of the road, with their children James and Frances.

Dave: I'm an engineer, and I run a business that makes environmental controls for buildings – high tech things that control heating, air conditioning and so on in houses, schools and factories. We work across the country, but the office is based in Uckfield. I set it up about eight years ago with a couple of other guys, and we employ about twenty-five people.

I've got a guilty secret in the garage. It's got lots of old motorbikes in it – seven or eight, I think, but I've lost count. It's interesting, because there are a lot of anti-car people around in Lewes. They're not vociferous in any way towards me, but I'm always acutely aware of what they're thinking as I chug around on this lovely old motor bike that I love very much. But I salve my conscience by reasoning that our business saves more energy than all these people spinning around in their cars.

The bandage on my hand? I lost control of the bike yesterday and took a tumble. It's very painful.

Polly: I did a music degree at Sussex, and followed it up with a piano diploma and post-graduate performing arts degree. I work as a teacher at Heathfield Community College, and sing with a choir based at Brighton University, which is directed by Andy Sherwood, who's based in Lewes. We've put on concerts at the Westgate chapel, where the choir really enjoyed the lovely building, acoustics and friendly audiences.

We bought this house four years ago, only a few days after it went on the market. The last family here had long since grown up, and Mrs Page – who was born at Rose Cottage – was now leaving the house. She looked pleased to see small children coming in the door, and she sold the house to us on the strict understanding that we would take care of Ben, the resident tortoise, who'd been bought for her son when he was small. Ben is now in his late forties, and still rummaging about the garden today.

It's a friendly street to live in, with a strong community spirit. In our second year here Christmas morning began for me at 8 o'clock when, on opening the door to go and collect the turkey from the garage, I found this knitted pillar box complete with holly leaf on top of the step. I was even more perplexed to see a knitted teddy Father Christmas on our letter box. Looking around the street I saw that every house down the bottom end had been decorated. It looked amazing, and I couldn't quite believe my eyes.

At about 3 o'clock in the afternoon we discovered that our neighbour Rebecca had been busy at seven that morning. She said she'd done it because, after all, this is St Nicholas Lane!

The bottom end of St Nicholas Lane west side.

Index

of Lewes people mentioned in the book